# BOUNDARIES AND BRIDGES

# BOUNDARIES AND BRIDGES

## Perspectives on Time and Space in Psychoanalysis

*Andrea Sabbadini*

**KARNAC**

First published in 2014 by
Karnac Books Ltd
118 Finchley Road
London NW3 5HT

British Library Cataloguing in Publication Data

A C.I.P. for this book is available from the British Library

ISBN-13: 978-1-78220-082-6

Typeset by V Publishing Solutions Pvt Ltd., Chennai, India

Printed in Great Britain

www.karnacbooks.com

*To Marta, Tommaso and Lorenzo*

# CONTENTS

# ACKNOWLEDGMENTS

Parts of this book contain passages taken from articles originally published elsewhere, or are revised versions of them, as from the following list. My gratitude goes to all the editors and publishers who have generously granted me their permission to use them here.

*The International Journal of Psychoanalysis* and Wiley
- Boundaries of timelessness: Some thoughts about the temporal dimension of the psychoanalytic space. *IJP, 70*: 305–313, 1989.

*Free Association*
- The year 2000: A psychoanalytic perspective on the fantasy of the new millennium. *FA, 9*: 56–71, 1987.

*The British Journal of Psychotherapy* and Blackwell Publishing
- Possession anxiety: The other side of the castration complex. *BJP, 3*: 5–13, 1986.
- How the infant develops a sense of time. *BJP, 5*: 475–484, 1989.
- Listening to silence. *BJP, 7*: 406–415, 1991.
- On sounds, children, identity and a "quite unmusical" man. *BJP, 14*: 189–196, 1997.

*Contemporary Psychoanalysis*
– The replacement child. *Cont. Psa,* 24: 528–547, 1988.

*Journal of the Society for Existential Analysis.*
– Treatment. *J.Soc. Exist. Analysis,* 2: 2–7, 1991.

*Psychoanalytic Review*
– On the open-endedness of psychoanalysis. *Psa. Rev.,* 94, 705–713, 2007.

Karnac Books Ltd. and Gabriela Goldstein
– In between and across. In: G. Goldstein (Ed.) (2013). *Art In Psychoanalysis: A Contemporary Approach to Creativity and Analytic Practice* (pp. 109–122). IPA Publications. London: Karnac.

Wayne State University Press and Tamar Jeffers McDonald
– The window and the door. In: T. Jeffers McDonald (Ed.) (2010). *Virgin Territory: Representing Sexual Inexperience in Film* (pp. 223–237). Detroit: Wayne State University Press.

# ABOUT THE AUTHOR

**Andrea Sabbadini,** *CPsychol*, is a Fellow of the British Psychoanalytical Society and its Director of Publications. He works in private practice in London, is a Senior Lecturer at UCL, a trustee of the Freud Museum, the director of the European Psychoanalytic Film Festival, and the chairman of a programme of films and discussions at the Institute of Contemporary Arts (ICA).

He is the founder editor of *Psychoanalysis and History* and the Film Section editor of *The International Journal of Psychoanalysis*. He has edited books on time, on paranoia, and on cinema, and is the author of *Moving Images* (Routledge), forthcoming in 2014.

# INTRODUCTION

*The chameleon darkens in the shade of him*
*who bends over to ascertain its colours.*

—Samuel Coleridge, 1817

This book consists of my attempt to distil some of the ideas which, in the course of almost forty years of psychoanalytic work, have emerged as foundations to my thinking and practice. Central among them are the theoretical concepts of time and space, and their significance in the different areas of my inquiry.

Before focusing on these concepts, however, I would like to share with my readers in more general terms some of my views about the meaning, practice and purpose of psychoanalytic work itself, as these inform much of what I will be talking about in the book. Because the language we use not only reflects but also fosters our attitudes, I will begin by pointing out that I never refer to my profession (other than when quoting other authors, Freud included) as a form of *treatment*— a term which I believe does not belong in the psychoanalytic vocabulary. I shall try to provide some justification for such a deliberate refusal to use a term that, as a quick perusal of our professional journals could easily demonstrate, is otherwise widely adopted by my colleagues.

For many years now the *Standard Edition of the Psychological Works of Sigmund Freud* has been criticised for its tendency to couch in over-clinical, pseudo-scientific language the original humanistic and philosophical content of Freud's ideas, but Strachey's translation of *Behandlung* as "treatment"[1] remains hardly questionable. It is true that the German term has connotations of a caring, attentive physical contact (involving touching with a hand: a procedure literally used by the father of psychoanalysis on his first patients' foreheads and later, for very good reasons, abandoned), while "treatment" has more sterile, distant, and coldly medical[2] overtones; but no better translation of that German word is available in English. The consequent medicalisation of our discipline, partly against Freud's own intentions,[3] has wide-ranging consequences on the ways in which psychoanalytic theory and practice are perceived by patients, therapists, and everyone else.

In the *Concise Oxford Dictionary* the verb "to treat" is given the following definition, among others: "*Deal with or act upon (person, thing) with view to obtaining particular result, apply process to, subject to chemical agent etc.*"[4] This definition may fit what some psychoanalysts do in their daily practice: they deal with or act upon their patients (persons or things) with a view to obtaining particular results, which they may or may not succeed in doing. They do treat patients who attend their consulting rooms in order to be treated, and therefore such therapists call what they do—in their minds, their conversations, their published articles and books—*treatment*. By using such language they implicitly, and sometimes explicitly, equate their therapeutic ministrations to those of dentists, psychiatrists and cardiologists. However, this is not what I believe psychoanalysis is about, nor is it what I do in my daily practice. I wish I could say that I intend to obtain a *particular result* or *apply a specific process* in my psychoanalytic work, but it would not be true. The term treatment does not describe the nature of what takes place in my consulting room. I do not think that I am treating anyone or anything.

I can almost hear now the voice of some respectable colleague (or is it my own?) saying: "All right, so you are not treating your patients, are you? Well, would you be kind enough to tell me what you do, then?" And he may even add for good measure, "… if anything?". I could try and defend myself by suggesting that I listen to people who come to see me and remember what they tell me; that I provide a safe enough environment for them; that I offer interpretations to their associations; that I take into account their defensive systems, their conflicts, their resistance to change, their pathological need to repeat destructive and self-destructive patterns of behaviour; that I pay attention to transference and countertransference phenomena … All of which, I hope, is true. But I know my interlocutor would not let me off the hook. "Bravo!", he could say, "So do I, but what for? What particular results do you intend to obtain by listening to your patients in a safe enough environment, offering transference interpretations, etc.? Because, surely, if you do not intend to obtain anything by doing that, then why do it at all?"

I know that I do not know how to answer that question. I keep asking it myself and keep coming up against my certainty that I do not treat the patients I see, that what I have to give them (*if anything*) is not treatment. Yet I am far from ready to jump to my respectable colleague's conclusion that if what I do, day in and day out, in my practice is not treatment, then it must be a waste of time, or a figment of my imagination.

We analysts, I would argue, follow certain principles, which of course undergo changes during our professional lives, but in the whole constitute a fairly solid body of knowledge, and a source of some certainty about what we do and for which purpose, and, therefore, of some security about who we are. We can classify, somewhat schematically, these guidelines under three partially overlapping categories. First of all we have *theoretical principles*, stemming from our therapeutic culture: our readings and studies during and after training, our discussions with colleagues, our own thinking. They provide us with models of mental structure and functioning, of psychological development and of interpersonal relationships. The following statements, for example, derive from a set of questionable, but not unreasonable, theoretical assumptions: "All dreams have a latent, unconscious meaning"; "Neurotic symptoms are overdetermined"; "Past object-relationships are often re-experienced in the here-and-now of the transference".

Then we have a number of *technical principles* based, like those in the first category, on our therapeutic culture, but also more specifically on our clinical experience, and on what we have learnt from our analysts, our supervisors and our mistakes. Their main function is to guide us in our daily practice, providing it with a certain amount of continuity and consistency. Most of us would agree, for instance, that it is not useful to get into arguments with patients, that their wishes should be interpreted rather than gratified, and that it is important to respect the time and space boundaries of the psychoanalytic setting.

Finally, we follow *ethical principles*, grounded in our own personal moral convictions, as well as on professional explicit or implicit codes of conduct. They give us both responsibilities and respectability, and are intended to protect those who use our services from gross physical, psychological and financial abuse. For example: confidentiality should be maintained; it is not acceptable to become sexually involved with our patients; and we should not see in analysis our own friends or relatives.

We must at this point ask ourselves whether psychoanalysts who follow these or other such guidelines normally also have a plan or project which they adhere to in the course of their practice. Do they have clearly stated aims they work towards? Do they try to obtain specific therapeutic results? I suggest—with a provocative edge and some embarrassment—that we do whatever we do with our analysands primarily because it is not inconsistent with our theoretical, technical, and ethical principles. In other words, we more or less know where we are coming from and we walk along pathways which we have learnt are practicable. We also know that our journey involves respecting boundaries and crossing bridges. But we must humbly confess that we do not really know where we are going. This uncertainty can be a source of personal and professional anxiety, from which some therapists attempt to protect themselves through defence mechanisms—from rationalisation to denial—while the real issues are left untouched.

I think it would be fair to say that in fact we are following, rather than leading, our patients in their convoluted and ambivalent search for the truth. It is, indeed, remarkable that analysts should refer at all to their relationship with patients as treatment in so far as this concept emphasises something being done to someone else, while the focus of the analytic process, and of other non-directive forms of psychotherapy, is on its interactive and dynamic quality: one from which both patient and therapist must emerge changed for the analysis to be considered successful. Furthermore, it is blatantly inaccurate to describe as treatment a process whereby the one who is allegedly treating (the analyst) takes a mostly passive, receptive, containing, holding attitude, while the one allegedly being treated (the patient) has a mostly active, penetrating, giving, sharing role. In fact, we all seem to be ready to regard the statement, "What takes place in analytic treatment is what active therapists do to passive patients", as a myth engrained in some of our patients' minds for some of their own pathological (depresssive) or perverse (masochistic) motives—a myth to be challenged through our interpretations in the course of their analysis. It is obvious, though, that we could not challenge this myth in others while holding on to it ourselves.

To return now to the crucial issue of whether or not we psychoanalysts know where we are going, perhaps it could be said that ultimately it does not matter as long as we stay with our patients. I was impressed by Bruno Bettelheim's suggestion, in the course of an interview, that when one of the troubled adolescents in his Orthogenic School ran away, Bettelheim would send a (fast) member of his staff to run *with* him—not *after* him! And not with the immediate aim of bringing the fugitive back, but to keep him company and make him feel that he was not alone. Apparently, both the runaway youngster and his escort always came back.

Ronald D. Laing—psychiatrist, psychoanalyst, philosopher, poet, and guru—is unlikely to be remembered in the history of culture for his contributions to psychiatry, psychoanalysis, philosophy, poetry, or guruism. But he will be remembered as a convincing demystifier, a fighter engaged in the demolition of some of the most deeply engrained myths in Western society—something we should all be grateful to him for. In fact, there are probably only two myths that R. D. Laing fell short of attacking: he never demystified R. D. Laing (though many others have done that for him) and he never demystified demystification. I am not concerned here about Laing's views on the use of legal drugs in orthodox psychiatry and illegal ones in therapy and in daily life, or about his understanding of normal and pathological (or pathogenic) communication, or about the knots couples and families entangle themselves with; and I will likewise not discuss here his contentious remarks about the sanity of psychotics and the madness of psychoanalysts.

I shall instead focus my attention upon Laing's powerful demystification of the psychotherapeutic process, upon his insistence on refusing to just treat people who were coming to him for treatment, and to collude with colleagues, including his many students, supervisees and followers, who were convinced that they were just treating patients. Indeed, he is still leading us today to question our own assumptions about what we do and why, ultimately helping us to abandon some of our narcissistic omnipotence. Why should sessions last fifty minutes, rather than half an hour, or three days? Why should the patient lie on the couch instead of sitting on a hand-woven Indian rug on the floor? (Indeed, why call him or her a patient in the first place?). Why should the therapist sit on a chair rather than, say, stand upside down in a yoga position? (Indeed, why call him or her a therapist in the first place?). "The psychotherapeutic relationship", wrote Laing, "is ... a research. A search constantly reasserted and reconstituted ... True, in the enterprise of psychotherapy there are regularities, even institutional structures, pervading the sequence, rhythm and tempo of the therapeutic situation viewed as process ... But the really decisive moments in psychotherapy, as every patient or therapist who has ever experienced them knows, are unpredictable, unique, unforgettable, always unrepeatable and often undescribable" (Laing, 1967, p. 47). Here, I do agree with him.

The question for me—for all of us involved in this profession, assuming we consider it to be more than just a job from which to earn a living and derive a sense of identity—is whether enough room is left for the theoretical, technical, and ethical principles of the kind I have referred to above. I am prepared to question and, if necessary, to change each one of the principles I presently adhere to in my practice, though not without some understandable resistance, of course. I am convinced that an analyst who fails to accept, or indeed to encourage, such a challenge, wherever it may be coming from, has stopped learning and growing— has, in other words, stopped being a good therapist.

I am not prepared, however, to do away with principles altogether, as some self-styled radical therapists advocate. They seem to believe that there is something wrong in principle with principles, without realising that principles are always present even when not explicitly stated, providing a structure and boundaries within which to operate. Without guidelines on how to behave, models of mental functioning and some understanding of the relationship between external and internal worlds, there can only be chaos, exploitation, meaninglessness, confusion, fragmentation, or emptiness—the very experiences that bring people to us in the first place. If we are willing to demystify our profession, it is not in order to reject it, but to improve and enrich it.

I often wonder if that suffering that is presented (offered, projected) to me day in and day out in my consulting room by those who come to see me, if not for treatment certainly for some sort of help, is closer to some ultimate human truth, however unbearable, or to a colossal form of self-deception. I have so far found no answer to such a crucial philosophical question—which underlies the related issues of treatment and change—and I am by nature or nurture far too sceptical to believe I will ever find it.

The problem is whether madness or psychopathology, for want of better terms to describe such suffering, is an uncompromising expression of some down-to-the-bone existential truth, or else its concealment. Either way, it is usually when its price has become too high that people consider entering analysis. We may not treat them, but we still have to face such dilemmas: whether to believe what is revealed bare in front of our eyes and ears as the truth—our patients' if not our own—or to expose it as a distortion, a perversion, a mask. Or, indeed, whether to consider it a compromise formation: a sophisticated solution, however painful, damaging and contradictory, to an impossible problem. To which our "impossible profession", as Freud himself once called psychoanalysis (and Laing would not have disagreed), can only tentatively attempt to make alternative, and not necessarily better, solutions available. There, whatever our theoretical, technical, and ethical principles, we must stop.

*  *  *

After this rather lengthy but hopefully not futile digression, I will now come back to a more direct description of the contents of this book, and of some of its theoretical foundations.

The dimensions of time and space provide the coordinates through which we perceive external reality on the one hand, and experience internal mental and emotional states on the other. *Time* plays a key role in psychoanalysis—a process which is always terminated, while being intrinsically interminable—because bringing about change is one of its main therapeutic functions and because the transference operates according to temporally determined mechanisms, such as regression and repetition, involving the actualisation of aspects of the past in the present. As to *space*, the existence of mental representations of external objects and object-relations involves the presence of an internal location where such representations occur. The complex interrelationships between inner and outer, as well as a definition of the borders separating them and of the bridges connecting them, are issues at the core of all psychoanalytic models of psychological functioning. In this book I endeavour to refer to some of the psychoanalytic concepts that have contributed to our understanding of these universally intriguing concepts, as well as to offer some of my own ideas about them.

*Chapter One: A sense of time* introduces the concept of a mono-dimensional "infantile omnipresent" to describe the original temporal experience in babies before they develop the capacities to remember the past and anticipate the future. Such an omnipresent state is related to the timeless quality of our unconscious life and is associated to the infant's narcissistic sense of omnipotence and still relative indifferen-tiation of the self from the external world. The development of a more mature sense of time involving the gradual acquisition of a differen-tiated past/present/future perspective is considered here in parallel with the acquisition of a sense of personal identity.

Problems in this area are explored in *Chapter Two: The replacement child*. It begins by considering the general condition of individuals whose sense of identity is undermined by the impression that they are not quite themselves—a condition related here to the Freudian category of the Uncanny and to the literary device of the double. An extreme instance of this phenomenon is represented by the "replacement child", here described with the help of a detailed analytic case. Replacement children are those conceived with the conscious purpose on the part of their parents to substitute a dead sibling. Such children inevitably suffer from a sense of confusion in the area of self-identity, and often display serious difficulties in the development of self-esteem and in the establishment of mature object-relationships.

*Chapter Three: The window and the door* further explores the issue of personal identity by examining the meaning of certain specific conflicts concerning the body and sexuality of young people. The main focus here is on the fantasies, fears, and desires associated to the issue of vir-ginity. Such conflicts are seen in a developmental context of young peo-ple's struggle with the wish to become grown-ups and conform to the identities of their parents' generation, and that of remaining dependent children. Themes of time, identity, and the boundaries of one's personal space, as well as issues about a private new relationship to one's body and a social one to one's peers, play a crucial part in how such a struggle is negotiated and resolved, or else fails to find a satisfactory outcome.

*Chapter Four: Boundaries of timelessness* examines the psychoanalytic situation itself from the perspective of its specific temporal structure. What emerges is a paradoxical "contrast of temporalities" between the rigorous time limitations imposed upon the setting by analytic technique, on the one hand; and, on the other, the atmosphere of timelessness so often characterising the experience of psychoanalysis, both as a whole and within individual sessions. The roots of this timelessness are traced back to unconscious primary process functioning and to the original experience of unidimensional time described in Chapter One.

The experience of time as a central aspect of the psychoanalytic situation for both analysts and patients is further examined in *Chapter Five: Open-endedness and termination*, where it is argued that not stipulating from the beginning a date for termination of analysis is one of its main features. Among other reasons, the freedom associated to its open-endedness can offer a better chance for the liberating and therapeutic experience of timelessness to take place in the course of the session. This, of course, does not mean that analysis (at least in the concrete sense of regular meetings between its two participants) should not eventually come to an end. Indeed, the termination phase itself is seen here as an essential component of the analytic process. This chapter also takes into account some of the criteria for deciding when to end an analysis, and some of the issues that may emerge in that delicate stage of the work.

Moving then to a temporal theme of wider historical and cultural implications, the next chapter, *The year 2000*, looks at how the recent transition from the second to the third millennium has occupied our fantasy lives. In particular, it examines the narcissistic significance of feeling "special" for belonging to a watershed time; the projection of internal objects onto a Golden Age; the omnipotent sense of immortality, stemming from living in neither millennium and in both; and, last but not least, the voyeuristic fantasies, related to primal scene wishes, of having access to a world where we do not belong. Reference is made to the grandiose and catastrophic predictions that dominated the minds of those who lived through similar experiences a thousand years ago, but also to the equally extreme, if often only unconscious, millenarian fantasies occupying the inner worlds of our contemporaries.

The question about the space, both concrete and metaphorical, where the analytic process unfolds is the subject of *Chapter Seven: On the couch*. The focus here is on that piece of furniture, the couch, on which, since Freud's days, analysands lie. Unlike most other professions psychoanalysis uses no tangible tools, and its only one, the couch, has become in the collective imagination the iconic symbol of everything we do in our consulting rooms. It will be argued here though, that what ultimately matters is not so much where patients place their bodies, but their conscious and unconscious reasons for doing so. These could be subsumed under the partially overlapping categories of sexuality, passivity and loss of control, and wishes and fears associated with seeing and being seen. Reference will also be made to the virtual space where new electronic technologies allow some analysts to conduct sessions from a distance.

Still in the area of what occupies and defines mental space, *Chapter 8: Possession anxiety* postulates the existence of a common source of anxiety which is conceptualised as the other side of castration anxiety. While the latter concerns the fear of the loss of a precious object, possession anxiety relates to the presence of an ambivalently charged one, over which the person possessing it will then fear losing control. Possession anxiety is symbolically represented by the phallus and is associated to the genital stage of development. It is examined here from the viewpoint of its temporal connotations and in its significance for the understanding of the transference.

The next two chapters deal from different perspectives with the importance of the auditory dimension in psychoanalysis. *Chapter Nine: Listening to silence* looks at the different silences, considered here as complementary to words, which always play a part in the analytic dialogue; and how an attempt to understand their complex and overdetermined emotional meanings (often going beyond the expression of resistance) may constitute an important part of the therapeutic process. The silent space within a session is considered as a sort of container of words and as a compromise formation concealing the unconscious fantasy from which it originates, while expressing a conscious one, often related to the transference situation.

In complementarity with the chapter about silence, *Chapter Ten: Listening to sounds* focuses on the importance of sounds and music (an exquisitely auditory experience, not unlike psychoanalysis itself) for human development. After a brief historical review of Freud's own ambivalent attitude to music, the chapter will consider here children's early relations to sounds. In particular, their sense of identity is seen as being formed through a process of "echoing" of the mother's voice, in parallel with the visual "mirroring" of her image.

The concluding chapter, *In between and across*, dwells on those metaphorical bridges that connect a variety of disparate mental and cultural phenomena. With reference to the metaphor of analysis as a journey, the chapter plays with the task of describing the meaning of gaps and intervals between events and between experiences—the transitional space/time separating them, as well as the metaphorical bridges that could join them. This approach may be applied to our clinical work (for instance in relation to our understanding of borderline conditions, of manic flights, of the transference, and of traumas), as well as to a number of cultural areas, such as those occupied by music or by cinema. The chapter, and with it the book, is concluded by some analytically informed observations on creativity and on the psychoanalytic work itself as a creative process.

\* \* \*

Before leaving the readers of this introduction to decide whether to embark upon reading also the pages following it, I would like to put forward a question which has occupied my mind many a time over the years and which I consider to be at the core of our understanding of human psychology. You will be hardly surprised to hear that I have to date found no satisfactory answer to it. This question presupposes a belief in the existence of that agency, timeless and without a location anywhere in space, which we call the unconscious—a belief I have held myself all my life and which I assume many of this book's readers may also share. The question, a secular version perhaps of the perennial theological debate over man's "free will", can be simply formulated as follows:

"Are we ultimately responsible for our unconscious?"

It would be easy to rush to an answer. "No, of course we are not! How could we possibly take personal responsibility for something we are not even aware of? How can we be blamed for the murderous content of our dreams when we would never conceive of committing such a crime in real life? How could we blame Oedipus for marrying a woman he could not know was his own mother?" Etcetera.

It would be equally easy, however, to rush to the opposite conclusion: "Of course we are responsible for our unconscious! Who else would be? Our parents? Society? God? Our good or bad luck? Like it or not, it's us, nobody else but us. It's our dreams even if we resist accepting their meaning; it's our symptoms much as we try to dismiss them. All we think and say and do, wherever it may come from, is ours and nobody else's, and therefore we should acknowledge our responsibility for it and, when appropriate, pay the price. Even the Thebans knew that much when they banned King Oedipus from their city." Etcetera.

Reading this book is unlikely to present you with a convincing and definitive answer to this question, much as writing it has not provided it to me. But I hope the following pages may help you move a little closer to understanding the richness of its implications.

## CHAPTER ONE

# A sense of time

O ur lives, like those of other animals, are immersed in the temporal dimension. But human beings, unlike other animals, are aware of it: we have a "sense of time".

What do we mean by sense of time? How do we develop such an awareness? How do we achieve a relatively consistent relationship to the temporal dimension of our existence? What happens to us if such a relationship is not properly established, or if it breaks down?

Rather than letting myself be drawn into the fascinating territory of philosophical speculations on these matters, I will focus here on the psychology of the development of the sense of time in the first months of the infant's life. In order to do this, I will refer to psychoanalytic concepts elaborated from child observation and from clinical work with adult patients. More specifically, I shall dwell on the parallel between the development of the sense of time in the child and her achievement of a sense of identity.

"All definitions of the self and of the sense of identity", writes Rycroft, "inevitably include a reference to time" (Rycroft, 1968, p. 167). It seems to me that it is a necessary condition for time to exist as a subjective *continuum*, that the person experiencing it has developed a sufficiently stable sense of identity; and, conversely, for identity to be formed and maintained, time should have acquired its distinctive qualities (i.e., succession, duration, and irreversibility) so that under normal conditions it can be experienced as a constant flow from past to future via the present.

At birth instincts, drives, and their gratification form a magically inseparable unit; according to the pleasure principle that dominates this earliest phases of life, all wishes are satisfied straightaway, by either real or hallucinatory means. In other words, the self is narcissistically omnipotent and the baby has no clear sense of identity: subject and object are an inseparable whole. For example, the baby experiences the maternal breast that satisfies his oral needs as an integral part of himself and cannot yet recognise the possibility of an interpersonal relationship. To quote from Jacobson: "At first the infant can probably hardly discriminate between his own pleasurable sensations and the objects from which they are derived" (1964, p. 39).

What then is the experience of time likely to be at the very start? Classical psychoanalytic theories about the formation of the first nucleus of temporal awareness—which link its origins to the different phases of the child's psycho-physical development and to her adaptation to the environment—cover a wide spectrum. According to Klein, the concept of time originates at birth. "It would appear", she writes, "that the change from intra-uterine to extra-uterine existence, as the prototype of all periodicity, is one of the roots of the concept of time and of orientation in time" (Klein, 1923, p. 99). For Liberman (1955), time is a form of object-relationship which begins in the moment between leaving the womb and the drawing of the first breath. For others the earliest experience of time is in the oral stage: "All that is most fundamental to a person's appreciation of time and rhythm originates in a pattern laid down at the breast period" (Yates, 1938, p. 354), while Hárnik (1925) believes that it will be later, in connection with defecation and the imposition of sphincter control, that the child first becomes aware of time. For Gifford the adaptation to the rhythm of sleep and wakefulness indicates the presence not only of a first precursor to the sense of time, but also of early ego-functioning, "because instinctual needs are modified in accordance with periodic changes in the environment" (Gifford, 1960, p. 6).

My suggestion is that at first the infant has no capacity to differentiate time in its past, present, and future dimensions. This narcissistically omnipotent baby lives immersed in what I can only describe as an *infantile omnipresent*; this is a mono-dimensional and all-embracing present that transcends the boundaries of time, because it ignores both the joys and suffering of memory and the anxiety of waiting.

It is to this kind of magical temporality that Lewis Carroll's Mad Hatter refers to when he advises Alice to keep on good terms with time:

> Suppose it were nine o'clock in the morning, just time to begin lessons: you'd only have to whisper a hint to Time, and round goes the clock in a twinkling! Half-past one, time for dinner! (Carroll, 1865, p. 92)

In order to understand the roots of this mono-dimensional time, it is useful to relate it to another concept, that of the timelessness of the unconscious, which Freud introduced in his description of the functioning of the mental apparatus. "In the Unconscious", he wrote, "nothing can be brought to an end, nothing is past or forgotten" (Freud, 1900a, p. 577); and again: "The processes of the system *Ucs.* are *timeless*; *i.e.*, they are not ordered temporally, are not altered by the passage of time; they have no reference to time at all" (Freud, 1915e, p. 187).

According to classical psychoanalysis, then, the unconscious is an undifferentiated and primitive psychical territory where temporal relations, if they exist at all, do not follow those laws of duration, succession, and irreversibility that condition our conscious life, and where repressed material is preserved without losing its original characteristics. This is apparent, for instance, in the manifest content of dreams, which often reflects the timeless qualities of the unconscious. One of the consequences of this formulation is that the unconscious, not admitting the presence of time or of anything negative within itself, does not believe in its own death and therefore "it behaves as if it were immortal" (Freud, 1915b, p. 296). At the conscious level, this belief involves the denial of the passing of time that manifests itself in the "illusion" of religions, and in the sublimated forms of language, culture and art. The unconscious, then, if we accept the principle of its timelessness, assumes a position of genetic priority; it manifests itself "as the primordial vital element, the basis of the being or the being itself … without a real beginning and without any intrinsic change …. It has no need for a specific historical dimension in order to survive" (Abraham, 1976, pp. 462–463). It is reasonable to assume that the infant, whose mental functioning follows the same principles of the unconscious primary process, should also experience a kind of time (the omnipresent) closely related to unconscious timelessness.

We have left our infant in a state of being narcissistically satisfied (in reality or in fantasy), and living in that mono-dimensional time which we have called the omnipresent. Very soon though, this young child is doomed to experience an inevitable delay in the satisfaction of her needs: in order to survive, the psychic apparatus must develop the capacity to postpone the fulfilment of wishes and to tolerate the resulting frustration. With the gradual establishment of the reality principle as the dominant (though by no means exclusive) mode of mental functioning, we can observe the beginning of a slow process of differentiation of the self from the not-self and of the internal world from the external one.

The delicate transition from an original state of undifferentiated fusion with the primary object to the subsequent stage of relative separation and individuation from it—when a first awareness of the self, or sense of identity, begins to take shape—witnesses to the gradual emergence of temporal and self-awareness. In particular, it is the dimension of psychological constancy to introduce a temporal perspective into our understanding of the establishment of self-identity.

Let me explain: the first nucleus of the sense of identity requires a capacity for object constancy—that is for relating to an internalised object and for maintaining it when the real one is absent. This capacity to tolerate frustration involves, in turn, a capacity to experience ambivalence in object-relationships. The object is no longer split, as it was at the beginning, between good (when present and satisfying) and bad (when absent and frustrating). The child can now understand that the mother he is relating to in the external world and in his fantasy is one and the same good and bad object, and not two different and separate ones.

In complementarity with the development of the capacity for object constancy, the sense of identity stems at first also from the establishment of self constancy, that is, from the capacity of the ego to experience itself ambivalently, to reflect upon itself, and to grow around a relatively strong core, unchanging in time and space. The child begins to feel that she is always herself, when she wakes up in the morning or goes to sleep in the evening, with her parents or alone, when happy or when upset. "The establishment of object and self constancy", writes Jacobson, "must be regarded as a very important prerequisite for … a healthy process of identification" (1964, p. 66), leading to the acquisition of the capacity to sustain lasting relationships with others and with oneself.

This process can otherwise be formulated as the achievement of a balance, under normal circumstances with no excessive tensions or conflicts, between the external time of the clock and the psychological time of one's needs. We can predict that when such a temporal balance is upset under pressure, the sense of identity is also threatened; and, conversely, when the sense of identity undergoes a crisis, the equilibrium of the two sets of time also becomes precarious.

The sense of identity can be considered as a consequence of a gradual resolution of the original narcissistic identification with the object, which is then a precondition for all later individuation. The concept of "mirroring", originally advanced by Lacan (1949) and then elaborated by Winnicott (1967) can be particularly useful in describing such a process. The child would discover his identity by looking into the face of his mother and identifying with her. "What does the baby see when he … looks at the mother's face?", asks Winnicott. His answer is that "what the baby sees is himself". But "many babies … have a long experience of not getting back what they are giving. They look and they do not see themselves" (Winnicott, 1967, p. 112).

In the well known Greek myth, Narcissus is followed by the nymph Echo, who is in love with him, while he falls in love with his own image, reflected in a pool of water. But both the reflected voice of the echo and the reflected image of the mirror take time to come back. It is in this very fraction of time—in this gap of waiting which Narcissus cannot tolerate and which leads to his tragic death—that change occurs: the reflection of the image and of the voice becomes a reflection of the ego on itself. Time and identity are once again closely associated.

The establishment of the capacity for object and self constancy is achieved through a process involving those transitional phenomena which Winnicott (1953) has described in connection with this stage of passage towards true object-relations. Whereas the "transitional object" represents a bridge in the process of separation from the self to the not-self,[1] the emergence of the sense of time would represent a bridge in the process of transformation from the temporally undifferentiated original world to the *real* world of becoming, movement, and change, which requires the postponement of the gratification of needs.

Let us now go back once again to our infant. What happens to her original, narcissistic, undifferentiated omnipresent, which we have seen to be so strictly related to her dependence on the pleasure principle, to her initial lack of sense of identity, and to her incapacity to differentiate herself from the external world?

As secondary process (preconscious and conscious) mental activities are established alongside primary process (unconscious) functioning; as the reality principle gradually replaces the pleasure principle; as primitive narcissism is forced to give up some of its omnipotence in order to establish object-relationships (by using transitional objects in a gradual process of separation and individuation from primary objects); as all these developments gradually occur, then the original, magically timeless omnipresent also undergoes a transformation into a multidimensional temporal perspective. This is of course possible as a result of, and in parallel with, the child's developing mastery of symbol formation processes and of language. "Greater capacity for symbolisation … makes possible the beginning differentiation of past, present and future. Memories, based on the capacity to retain representations of experience, come to signify past. The ability to anticipate interaction with objects … signifies the future" (Colarusso, 1987, p. 122).

It would be futile to get lost in the controversy as to whether the sense of past develops in the child before or after the sense of future, as there are good arguments supporting both views.

According to one of these theories, the omnipresent first opens up into a more realistic present time, where the discomfort of the still unsatisfied need prevails, and a future time characterised by the fantasy of gratification; the child will learn in a later phase the concept of past, which will take the configuration of a defensive regression in relation to the already established sequence of present/need—future/satisfaction. Hartocollis supports this view:

> A primitive sense of time emerges out of the awareness of change as experienced during the interval of suspenseful waiting that is defined by the perception of rising inner tension and the arrival of a wishfulfilling object. … The sense of future, as a function of the experience of anxiety, develops before the sense of 'pastness', which grows as a function of subjective memory and the sense of guilt or concern. (Hartocollis, 1974, p. 257)

A different view emphasises a genetic priority of the development of the sense of the past over the future, by maintaining that the achievement of the reality principle depends upon a memory of a previous satisfaction and that the delay of gratification, which is related to the future, results from that memory.

Ultimately, these two theories must be seen as complementary; the various temporal dimensions are the result of progressive differentiations from the original narcissistic omnipresent state, which we have seen to be intrinsically related to unconscious timelessness, in the same way that object-relationships are the result of progressive differentiations from the original fusion of the self with the external world.

* * *

What happens when the normal process of development of the sense of time and identity, as I have described it above, is impaired? When we come across a fixation at an intermediate stage in this psychological evolution? When adult experience and behaviour reveal a regression to such a point of arrest? When the originally achieved differentiation of the self from the outside world, and of time in a harmonious flux, becomes again nebulous fusion or psychotic confusion? When the boundaries become rigid, as in Muybridge or Marey's anatomical chronophotographies, or dissolve as in Salvador Dalí's melting watches?

I suggest that problems in the experience of either the sense of time or the sense of identity are reflected in forms of psychopathology that affect them both. The following fragment of clinical material from the analysis of Kate,[2] an artist with a borderline personality, might illustrate this point.

Kate is thirty-one years old. She has experienced a sense of despair since she was four. At thirteen her family was, in her own words, "a ship to be sunk", at sixteen it sank. She wears a heavy black jumper with blue jeans, and has a fringe. Around Kate's neck hangs a chain-watch that looks rather like the stopwatch of an Olympic Games umpire and which makes the noise of a kitchen alarm clock. She goes around saying that time must cool off, freeze off, be stopped by her in order to let her reach the world that surrounds her and which has left her behind. Kate feels she is travelling on a wrong train, of which she has forgotten the past station stops and ignores the future ones. Or, rather, she is waiting on the anonymous platform of a provincial station for a train that might never arrive. While waiting, she reads a newspaper, buys a sandwich, drinks a cup of coffee. With no determination or hope. Maybe, she thinks, it is already too late.

Kate would like all calendars of the universe to stop and let her recover the opportunities missed during all these years. Her internal world is dissonant with the external one. Boundaries are blurred. It is only through omnipotent magic that she kindles the illusion of arresting if not the inexorable flowing of life towards death, at least her own desperate sense of isolation and loneliness. Kate's identity in time is out of phase; for her it is like going to the theatre after the show has already begun and she is left with the sensation that there is always something missing that has happened before, something for her to catch up with, and yet something that is unreacheable in so far as it is past and finished.

The time of her sessions with me is always too short for her; in her experience a time that has had no beginning can have no end. "You always expect me", she shouted out of frustration at the end of a session, "to come here on time, to leave on time and to keep alive in between!".

She had wanted to 'phone me the previous night, to let me know about her despair; but then she had thought that I was likely to say: "We can talk about it when you come to see me tomorrow," and so she decided that, if everything always happens "tomorrow", it wasn't worth the effort. If only she could for an instant petrify time, like Zeno stopped Achilles so that he would not reach the tortoise, her mother would be with her for an eternity to satisfy her needs. But the hands of the clock already start their movement again …

In the next chapter I will refer to a series of conditions, both normal and pathological, the phenomenology of which is centred around the experience of "not being oneself", a variation of which is the condition of "being somebody else". A difficulty in the area of object and self constancy, in acquiring or maintaining a sense of identity, in the experience of time as a multidimensional *continuum*, and in keeping the self contained within the boundaries of one's physical and psychological body, is what such diverse experiences have in common. Among them are depersonalisation and derealisation, the fantasy of not being one's parents' child, the impression of living in a dream, or that of only existing in symbiotic complement with somebody else.

An extreme instance of this phenomenon is represented by the "replacement child", that is, a child conceived with the conscious purpose on the part of his parents of substituting a dead sibling. Replacement children inevitably suffer from a disturbance or a sense of confusion in the area of self-identity, and in their experience of themselves and others as constant in time. Furthermore, they often display serious difficulties in the development of self-esteem and in the establishment of mature object relationships. In the next chapter I shall report in some detail the case of Renate, a psychoanalytic patient who had been born nine months after the death of her nine-month-old sister Angela.

I shall now pull together some of the above considerations and draw some conclusions from them. We have looked at child development from the viewpoint of a gradual establishment of a sense of identity, and of the experience of time as a relatively constant flow within a three-dimensional perspective, by analysing the gradual passage from:

a. an original undifferentiated stage, characterised by a predominance of primary process functioning under the control of the pleasure principle, by an omnipotent narcissism stemming from a lack of clear differentiation of the self from the object, and by the experience of time as omnipresent, with little room as yet for a past to be remembered and a future to be anticipated. Through:

b. an intermediate stage of transitional object-relationships (Winnicott) and progressive separation and individuation (Mahler), with the emergence of object constancy (a capacity to feel ambivalence towards others and more tolerance to frustration through internalisation of objects) and of self-constancy (a first nucleus of self-identity in space and in time, a strengthening of the ego, and a first demarcation of boundaries between self and other). Towards:

c. a later stage that will represent the core of normal adult development, characterised by the predominance of secondary process functioning and of the reality principle—a clear differentiation of the self from the object which makes it possible for object-relationships and a sense of identity to be established and maintained; and by the experience of time as a *continuum* past-present-future flow. Under normal circumstances, external, objective, chronological time, and internal, subjective, psychological time, will then be in a state of balance, with no experience of them as differing or being in a state of tension or conflict with each other.

| Predominance of | Gradual establishment of |
|---|---|
| *Primary process functioning* ⟶ | *Secondary process functioning* |
| (incl. unconscious timelessness) | (incl. conscious sense of time) |
| *Pleasure principle* ⟶ | *Reality principle* |
| (immediate gratification of needs) | (postponement of gratification of needs) |
| Transitional objects (Winnicott) | |
| *Primary narcissism* ⟶ | *Object-relationships* |
| Separation–individuation (Mahler) | |
| *Fusion self/outside world* ⟶ | *Differentiation from the environment* |
| *Lack of object and self constancy* ⟶ | *Object and self constancy* |
| First awareness of time (anticipation and memory) | |
| *Infantile omnipresent* ⟶ | *Present/future/past time perspective* |
| (mono-dimensional time) | (three-dimensional time) |

I have postulated that alterations or disturbances in normal development affect later experiences of time and identity, as reflected in various psychopathological conditions. I have presented some clinical material from a borderline patient showing a sense of temporal and self-alienation from the world, and I have introduced the predicament of individuals who feel they are not quite themselves, such as, the replacement children—illustrating difficulties in these areas.

\* \* \*

It is the sense of time, then, that seems to provide an important link between the deeper layers of mental functioning and the first stages of our development.

Psychoanalytic theories of child development emphasise the dynamic nature of growth in human beings. The differentiation of the outside world from the self is a gradual, slow and inevitably uncompletable process. Much as the child does not move abruptly from the oral to the anal stage of psychosexual organisation, or from the paranoid-schizoid to the depressive position, and as we never entirely abandon the pleasure principle in favour of the reality one, so one can easily recognise relics of primary narcissism in all adults.

We can hardly feel surprised, then, if the picture we are confronted with is a complex and contradictory one. We shall find that the unconscious is not absolutely timeless; that in our conscious life we often seem to disregard time, its passage, and its limitations; that the experience of time in early childhood, though centred around what I called a narcissistic omnipresent, soon assumes a deeper temporal perspective that involves anticipation of the future and memory of the past; that in our adult life we sometimes behave as if past and future have no meaning, and all that matters is restricted to the present; the experiences of being in love or in acute physical pain illustrate this relative regression to a more mono-dimensional temporal perspective, as well as to a provisional loss of sense of identity.

The mental creations of young children, more than anything else, help us to appreciate the intimate similarities between their experience of life embedded in a relative omnipresent and the functioning of our unconscious mind, characterised by primary process logic and its timelessness. Children's words, their dreams, their fantasies, even their drawings, and the deep resonance they have for us adults, might bring us closer to understanding the origins and meaning of time for all of us.

## CHAPTER TWO

# The replacement child

U pon awakening, a man who has dreamt of being a butterfly wonders whether he is not a butterfly dreaming of being a man. In this paradox, ontology merges with epistemology: being and knowledge cannot be separated. Indeed, all knowledge *is* being and *is about* being. As in the Socratic "Know thyself" carved on the pediment of the temple in Delphi, all we really want to know is who we are—a wish related to our infantile, and never entirely satisfied, sexual curiosity about our origins.

It is maybe because none of us can be absolutely certain about our identities that we are all vulnerable to experiencing gaps in our sense of continuity in time and space, and to the disturbing sensation of "not being quite ourselves".

The uncanny sensation of not being oneself is so common in its numerous forms that probably all human beings experience it at some point in their lives. Yet—like the memory of a vivid dream vanishing early in the morning, just when one felt closest to grasping it—its ultimate essence must escape us.

Literature, philosophy, and psychology have made countless attempts to portray and conceptualise such phenomena, as they seem not only to have a universal quality, but also to be at the very foundation of our existence. I shall just mention here some of the many shapes in which these experiences can manifest themselves: depersonalisation, of which the pathological condition of multiple personality is the most extreme form; the related phenomenon of derealisation, beautifully exemplified by Freud's disturbance of memory on the Acropolis (Freud, 1936a); the fantasy of not being one's parents' child, for instance, through adoption, artificial insemination, or because the "real" baby was replaced in the cot with another one[1]; the sense—often bordering on either ecstatic or psychotic states—of living in a dream; a series of conditions that could be grouped under the category of "the double", whereby one feels that one exists in symbiotic complement with somebody else, with a twin or imaginary friend who is the mirror-image of oneself. What all of these diverse experiences have in common, is a difficulty—temporary or permanent as the case may be—in acquiring or maintaining a sense of identity, and in keeping the self contained within the boundaries of one's physical and psychological body.

The feeling of not being oneself has some of the qualities and connotations of that other wide category of psychological phenomena described by Freud (1919h) as *das Unheimliche* ("the uncanny") and characterised by a dissociative process in the ego.

In our case, what appear to be uncanny are elements of the external world onto which people project split-off fragments of their dissociated selves. This can eventually lead to disturbances in the process of psychological development, reality-testing, and object-relationships. I think that at the origin of such dissociative phenomena there is a failed adaptation, specifically in the area of identification with a good object: either because such an object was missing from the child's physical or emotional universe, or because she is unable for some reason or other to relate to it. Alternatively, the dissociation in the ego can be conceptualised as a pathological regression to a developmental stage preceding ego-integrity and ego-constancy.

For a different psychogenetic approach to the understanding of the roots of dissociation, we could turn to what Winnicott (1967) has described with the "mirror stage" metaphor. Without a mirror, that is, without a good-enough mother in whose eyes the child can recognise the forming reflection of his own image, the development of a sense of identity is impaired. As a result, the child will be unable to rely on the outside world for a sense of security and consistency, while the inner world, not having formed around a solid core, will become fragmented.

The person does not feel whole, or only feels an illusory wholeness by experiencing the environment as an inconsistent world of uncanny, bizarre objects with no continuity in space and time, constantly threatening to collapse.[2]

To illustrate one of these phenomena, here somewhat artificially grouped under the one category of "not being oneself", I shall refer to the "replacement child" syndrome. By definition, all children born to parents who have already lost a child are replacements, inasmuch as they are invested with expectations, projections, and displacements belonging to the dead one. This phenomenon is more noticeable in our days than it was at a time when infant mortality was higher, large families were the norm, and children were customarily born in close succession. In the present chapter, however, I shall restrict the term "replacement" to the child who has been conceived with the *conscious* purpose on the part of one or both parents of replacing another child who died a short time earlier. This substitute child, I believe, will be treated more as the embodiment of a memory than as a person in her own right.

If we follow this narrower definition, we cannot, for instance, include the case of already existing children substituting their parents' friends or other members of the family (as is often the case amongst survivors of massacres, concentration camps, or natural disasters), nor that of babies already conceived at the time of the death of a child in the family, although in this situation the living child is likely to become a replacement for the dead one—the more so the younger the dead child was.[3]

In the proper cases of child replacement, as opposed to those belonging to a looser definition, the conscious and unconscious emotional investment is more specific, and the psychological consequences for the new child more extreme. I cannot say whether such consequences are always pathological, but I believe that any child conceived, born and brought up under these circumstances will develop serious problems in the area of self-identity, and experience intense difficulties, particularly at the critical separation–individuation stage and during adolescence.

In all the six cases of replacement children they studied, Cain and Cain found that "the attempt to 'replace' was totally dominated by the image and memories of the dead child. It was perhaps most vividly demonstrated by one set of these parents who initially went to adoption agencies after their loss, requesting an eight-year-old, thin, blue-eyed, blond boy to replace their dead eight-year-old, thin, blue-eyed, blond boy" (Cain and Cain, 1964, p. 445). These authors identified two prominent features in the families of such children: what they call the premorbid personalities of the mothers (depressive, phobic, or compulsive) and the parents' excessive narcissistic investment in the children who had died. As a result, the substitute "was born into a world of mourning, of apathetic, withdrawn parents, a world focussed on the past and literally worshipping the image of the dead" (Cain and Cain, 1964, p. 445).

In his *Unspeakable Confessions* Salvador Dalí tells us how he was born into such a world:

> I lived through my death before living my life. At the age of seven my brother died of meningitis, three years before I was born. This shook my mother to the very depths of her being. This brother's precociousness, his genius, his grace, his handsomeness were to her so many delights; his disappearance was a terrible shock. She was never to get over it. My parents' despair was assuaged only by my own birth, but their misfortune still penetrated every cell of their bodies. And within my mother's womb, I could already feel their *angst*. My foetus swam in an infernal placenta. Their anxiety never left me … I deeply experienced the persistence of [my brother's] presence as both a trauma—a kind of alienation of affections—and a sense of being outdone. (Dalí & Parinaud, 1973, p. 12)

Renate, the psychoanalytic patient who provided me with most of the clinical material on which this chapter is based, had since childhood had serious psychological problems centring on her lack of sense of identity. Suffering from attacks of acute depressive anxiety, she came to analysis in her late thirties, in the hope of receiving help in dealing with her low self-esteem and sense of failure in her relationships.

Early in her therapy Renate told me that she had been born exactly nine months after the death of a nine-month-old sister. I shall here call this sister Angela, though I do not know her real name, nor do I know whether Renate herself knows it as she has never referred to her dead sister by name. I have wondered about the accuracy of this chronological detail: was it *exactly* nine months after Angela's death that Renate was born? In this case, it would be likely that she had been conceived very near the day when her sister had died. In fantasy this could mean that the sexual intercourse responsible for Renate's conception had taken place at the same time as Angela's death. Renate's mother told her that Angela had died from a respiratory illness and that drugs that could have saved her young life were not available in the hospital where she was treated. There was also a suggestion of a delay in medical intervention, due to negligence on the part of the parents or of the hospital staff.

Renate's low self-esteem, as manifested in the transference, could then be interpreted as being to a large extent the result of an ambivalent identification with her mother. This woman was an object of love (for having given her life) whom at the same time Renate deeply distrusted for having been incapable not only of preventing her first child's death, but also of mourning her loss and containing her own pain other than by producing a replica of that daughter. Renate told me that apparently her mother greatly rejoiced twice: first when she discovered that she was pregnant again, and then when the baby—"a real gift from God" as she put it—turned out to be another girl.

Of course, attempting to replace a dead child and rejoicing at succeeding in doing so can also be a mature, creative, and altogether positive means available to parents to deal with their loss and their pain. Often, though, and certainly in Renate's family, this decision is rather an indication of an immature way of coping with an emotionally unbearable life event, of a poor adaptation to reality (however catastrophic it might be) and of a pathological use of primitive defence mechanisms, such as omnipotent denial and displacement. In this sense, it would probably be more accurate to talk about *displacement* children than about replacement ones.

Let us go back to our reconstruction of the events. The story goes that when, after a few days of agony, Angela eventually died, her mother burst into desperate tears. The nun who was in charge of the nursing staff of the ward came to her and told her to be "brave" and to stop "all that nonsense". Every day young soldiers died in that hospital (these events took place during World War II) and those were real tragedies, the nun said, not the death of a baby. "And anyway", she apparently added with a comforting smile, "when children die they become angels!"

Again, I cannot know whether that statement was actually made (though it would not surprise me if it was) nor whether Renate's mother, a devout Catholic, believed it. Apparently, though, she stopped crying and it seems that the normal process of mourning for the death of her child was thus interfered with. By replacing her dead daughter with a live one, Renate's mother was replacing mourning with pregnancy.

A detailed assessment of Renate's mother's personality and possible pathology would only be speculation on my part, since Renate's experience of her, as it also manifested itself in the transference and the countertransference, was confused, ambivalent, and contradictory. I could only say that, from Renate's account of these crucial events, her mother emerged to my eyes as the tragic compound of psychological immaturity and the inescapable destiny of a true *Mater Dolorosa*.

What Renate has told me about Angela over the years of her analysis has always been rather foggy, uncertain, and confused. The fact that the issue of her dead sister was hardly ever explicitly mentioned in Renate's analysis, though it was constantly present in the transference, reflects the veil of silence—with all its undertones of guilt—that surrounded it in her family. And yet, of course, much as the dead girl was a continuous presence in the family, she was unmistakably there in the analysis as well. Let me illustrate this point with some clinical material from the fifth year of Renate's analysis.

After I had cancelled a Friday and Monday session, Renate spends some time on the following Tuesday and Wednesday exploring the fantasy that during my long weekend I have gone back to Italy to attend the funeral of a relative. On Thursday morning, she starts her session by saying that there was "something unwelcoming" in my facial expression when I went to collect her from the waiting room. She then says that I also looked sad, and she explains it by speculating that my previous patient must have told me something that I had found upsetting. I join in my mind her present comments about my "unwelcoming" and "sad" expression with the funeral material of the previous days, and ask her what this reminds her of. She immediately mentions Angela, for the first time in over two years: how sad her mother was throughout Renate's childhood—and how unwelcoming she experienced her to be—because of the previous girl having left her with so much unworked-through pain. Renate then goes on to repeat, with some new details added, various anecdotes and myths about Angela's death, and her mother in relation to it, that she had already told me about in the first two years of her analysis.

The main interest for us here is the way in which the original traumatic situation is repeated *pari passu* in the transference. Again we find a bereaved mother (the sad analyst) who replaces mourning with pregnancy, but then discovers that she is unable to care for her daughter (the analyst, unwelcoming to his present patient), as he is still emotionally preoccupied with his lost child (the previous patient).

*  *  *

The nun's prophecy that Renate's sister would become "an angel" fulfilled itself. This angel, or ghost, never left the family again. Renate, more than anyone else, was affected by it, and her personality and psychopathology still bear the marks of that intangible presence. "The image of the dead child", write Cain and Cain paraphrasing Freud, "casts its shadow upon his replacement" (Cain and Cain, 1964, p. 451).

Renate at times experienced this angel as a protective presence, at other times, maybe more often, as a persecutory one. Certainly she could never get away from it, as from the day of her conception it had become the "secret sharer" of her life; it had penetrated her as an intrinsic component of her existence, as an unavoidable thread woven into the very fabric of her destiny.

Intermingled with a sense of omnipotent triumph, guilt plays a major role here. Had Angela not died, Renate would not have been conceived, and so her life depended on her sister's death. The leap from this to the conviction that she must have killed her sister in order to come into existence herself is, for the unconscious, a small yet crucial step. It is interesting in this respect that, in her twenties, Renate trained as a paediatric nurse and for a time worked in a ward of terminally ill babies. In her analysis she became aware of her deep-rooted reasons for making such a professional choice, which included a series of identifications (with the mother, the nun, the dead sister, and the surviving baby, *i.e.,* herself); the attempt at reparation of the broken object—lost, imprisoned or dead inside her mother and herself; and the sadistic and voyeuristic needs to observe the deaths of babies over and over again, in compulsively futile attempts to assuage her guilt and relieve her suffering.

I also wonder if Renate's decision to have an abortion when she found herself pregnant some thirty years later may have been the expression (through identification with her mother) not only of a fear of having a baby who would have been damaged and who would have died like Angela, but also of experiencing her own pregnancy as a form of grief for the lost sister. If so, it was in order to avoid getting in touch again with that loss that Renate had to bring about another death through the termination of her pregnancy. With the help of denial and rationalisations, Renate avoided feeling any grief. For many weeks she did not consciously realise that she was pregnant; then, in a state of numbness, she decided to have the abortion. She felt nothing during or after the procedure and she did not say a word about it to anybody, not even to her boyfriend. It was only many years later, in her analysis with me, that for the first time she brought the whole episode to the surface and began to belatedly experience some of the affects—anger, sadness, grief, guilt, and remorse—that she had not felt at the time.

Who is the angel, who is the ghost? The dead sister inside her, or she inside the dead sister? How can Renate be herself under such psychological circumstances? How can she be a whole object and develop a unique sense of identity? And if she can then be only a part-object—the other "part" of it being buried with the dead sister whom she has never met—then her mother too could be only a part-object, who can give Renate only part of her love, part of her attention, part of her time: just like me in the transference. The other part was forever bound to an invisible and, for this very reason, unbeatable ghost, "as the air, invulnerable" (Shakespeare, *Hamlet*, I, 1).

This introduces us to the central problem of sibling rivalry. The questions change now: How could Renate compete with an absent object? How could she fight a ghost constantly idealised in the form of an angel? How could she live up to a model existing only in her mother's mind? The rivalry with her dead sister was further complicated by the birth, some three years later, of another girl. From early on in her life Renate was expected to look after her sister, but she could only do so with extreme emotional difficulties, as her competitive and murderous feelings toward her younger sister—as well as her identification with her as "younger sister" in relation to Angela—were constantly coloured with the ambivalence and the guilt pertaining to the dead one.

At times Renate, as a child, did not even dare ask her mother for a hug, because she felt her mother had to preserve her affection for her younger, sicklier, and more demanding daughter, who got most of it for herself then, as she still does now. In Renate's experience, there was not enough love and understanding to go around in their family: only a limited amount was available, and she was not even allowed to have a fair share of it. We now know that, behind the younger live sister, we could discern the shadow of the older dead one, securing her large portion of motherly love away from Renate. Thus, my patient found herself squeezed between these two sisters, fighting for her mother's attention on two fronts: in the daylight with her actual sibling, and in darkness with a ghost. Her search for sufficient breathing space in which to develop her own autonomous self was doomed to fail. This fight for external as well as inner space became for Renate a never-ending and frustrating endeavour. Her priority became finding an identity, a sense of belonging, a place in society, a feeling of deserving to be who she was, and to keep what she had, and to mean something in her own right to others.

Until she came into analysis, and for a long time afterwards, Renate's world was a shaky universe of uncertainties, where she and others around her were constantly searching for boundaries, struggling for a place where they could belong, feeling alienated from themselves and each other, looking for an identity they could not find, because its core was somewhere else. I think that this "incapacity to be oneself" could be related to what Winnicott (1958) described as the "capacity to be alone" in the presence of the mother. Precisely because, from the day she was conceived in her mother's mind and womb, Renate always had to share her space with an uncomfortable guest/ghost, she could not develop that capacity to be alone, which is a precondition for the development of a sense of identity and of the capacity to be with others. In order to cope with this kind of situation, a child might elaborate to an abnormal degree some specific fantasies that are also common in children without major problems of identity; for instance, that a "double" exists somewhere that is one's authentic self, and of which one is only a shadow or a dim mirror reflection. This double has strong narcissistic connotations and, as "immortal self", it has the function of defending the ego from the fear of death and annihilation. Having already died, Angela (Renate's double) provided her with an aura of immortality that like a talisman would magically protect her from her own destructive and self-destructive impulses.

Renate's own fear of death apparently overwhelmed her during the weeks preceding her menarche. She remembers that she could not go to sleep, feeling terrified that she would never wake up again. Only her mother lying down next to her would relieve her anxiety. With the first menstruation, this terror disappeared overnight. Renate's mother had felt particularly upset by the fact that Angela had died at an age (nine months) when she was becoming independent—crawling away from her and playing by herself—and it had been painful for her to see this developmental process so suddenly interrupted. In this connection, Renate's fear of death before her first menstruation was also associated to an unconscious identification of her sister's lethally dangerous step towards independence in the separation–individuation phase (becoming a toddler) with Renate's own traumatic introduction to adolescence—to a time in her life, that is, when she would become capable of bearing real children of her own without needing to borrow her mother's womb any more to produce fantasy babies. Once the dangerous transitional period was over (with menarche) the intensity of the identification with the dying sister was lessened, and Renate's own fear of death could subside and be repressed again.

Of course such fear found other, if less dramatic, forms of expression. One that played a central role in Renate's analysis was her dread of silence. Silences—in a group of friends, in an evening class, or in a session with me—were for her paralysingly painful situations, which she felt entirely responsible for and incapable of putting right. Gradually the meaning of such fear became understandable, as Renate remembered from her early childhood how her mother, being often very quiet and depressed, made her feel that she had to talk to her in order to cheer her up. For Renate, the silence represented both the mother's mourning and the dead sister herself, whose missing voice Renate was anxious to replace. (The different meanings of silence in analysis will be explored in more detail in Chapter Nine.)

Her relationship with her mother remained a difficult one. Renate's complaints to me about her were centred around her conviction that her mother talked all the time about herself, as if Renate did not exist or as if she were someone else. Apparently, her mother never asked Renate what she did or how she felt, as if she had to pretend that Renate did not exist in her own right, as if she should not know who Renate really was. Renate extended this view of her mother's indifference—treating her as if she were in herself irrelevant and almost unreal, being just a substitute of someone else—to almost everybody else, including of course myself. People, she claimed with a rationalising generalisation, are selfish; they only want to talk about themselves, with no interest or respect for anyone else. Realising that I, unlike her mother, did listen to her, hour in and hour out, without ever talking about myself, has been for years a source of great puzzlement to Renate and of suspicion as to my hidden motives.

During a session, Renate heard in the background some music coming from downstairs. She suddenly remembered a long-forgotten episode from her late childhood. Her mother is in the kitchen, the radio, as usual, is on, playing some light music. Renate is sitting at the kitchen table doing her homework. As her mother leaves the room, Renate retunes the radio to a station of classical music. When her mother comes back, she gets angry with Renate: "What is this? It sounds like funeral music!"

I have already indicated that the theme of her dead sister, with all its variations, myths and anxieties surrounding it, was a taboo in Renate's family, and consequently in her analysis too. In the countertransference I was often left to fantasise and guess about it, feeling as curious about its details and meanings as Renate must have felt herself as a child.[4] In this area, my interpretation of the clinical material had, more than ever, a speculative quality. It was only when Renate's extreme sense of alienation (in the literal sense of the word, of feeling separate from oneself, feeling a distressing split in one's sense of identity, having the impression of being "someone else") became apparent in the context of the transference that I really felt certain as to where from the past the present experience was drawing its emotional intensity.

I have referred to such an instance: when Renate saw me as "sad" and "unwelcoming" to her, and preoccupied with someone else, like her mother had been throughout her childhood. I had another vivid illustration of the effect on the transference of Renate's peculiar status as a replacement child when, after nearly six years, we started considering termination of her analysis. When the time came to make the decision (and it would have made little difference had such a time come any earlier or later) Renate could only experience it as premature, as Angela's death—and Renate's own birth, or rather conception—had been. As I had expected, Renate perceived anything I said about the ending of her analysis as evidence of my wish to get rid of her because she had done something wrong. In this respect, I think she was reliving in the transference the continuous rejections by her mother for being so inadequate in comparison with the idealised Angela.

In this context, something interesting also happened to my countertransference. Not long before the issue of Renate's termination of analysis had come up, my ex-analyst had asked me if I had any vacancies, as he had recently interviewed a prospective patient whom he would have liked to refer to me for analysis. I was flattered by his offer, but had to refuse, having no times available. However, as soon as Renate and I started talking about the forthcoming end of her therapy, and long before we could even think of arranging a date for it, I considered asking my colleague to refer his patient to me, thus repeating in the countertransference the predicament of Renate's mother (asking "God" for the gift of a "replacement") without giving myself the time for a proper mourning process.

\* \* \*

Otto Rank (1925), in his excellent review of the many variations on the theme of the *double* to be found in folklore, literature, and anthropology, emphasises the narcissistic significance of this motif in relation to the idea of death and to infatuation with one's own image.[5]

Literature abounds with powerful descriptions of *der Doppelgänger*: Edgar Allan Poe's short story *William Wilson* (1839); Dostoyevsky's early novel *The Double* (1846); *The Secret Sharer* (1910), one of Joseph Conrad's masterpieces; Arthur Schnitzler's *Casanovas Heimfahrt* (1917).[6] Besides, the double as narrative device has also been traditionally much exploited in drama and film.[7]

"The most prominent symptom of the forms which the double takes", writes Rank, "is a powerful consciousness of guilt which forces the hero no longer to accept the responsibility for certain actions of his ego, but to place it upon another ego, a double" (Rank, 1925, p. 76). Freud points to a possible development of the double into what later became the ego-ideal and the superego. He writes:

> The idea of the "double" does not necessarily disappear with the passing of primary narcissism, for it can receive fresh meaning from the later stages of the ego's development. A special agency is slowly formed there, which is able to stand over against the rest of the ego, which has the function of observing and criticizing the self and of exercising a censorship within the mind, and which we become aware of as our "conscience". (Freud, 1919, p. 235)

Sometimes the *doppelgänger* takes the form of an imaginary companion (see Nagera, 1969) or of a twin. Here, splitting and projection play prominent roles: the double thus becomes the dumping ground of both idealisations and denigrations. In Renate's case, her dead sister becomes the model that cannot be equalled but must be loved, as well as the persecutory ghost to be destroyed.

This particular configuration also lends itself to an omnipotent pseudo-resolution of the Oedipus complex. The dead sister becomes the object of libidinal and aggressive instincts or, alternatively, she becomes the mother's partner, leaving the young girl free to relate to her father. In this respect, Renate reported what was probably the only good memory about him: going peacefully to sleep in his lap, while her mother was in the kitchen isolating herself into her depressive thoughts, presumably about Angela.

Incidentally, Renate's father's near-total absence from this chapter is only a reflection of his distance from his family life, his lack of involvement with his children, his apparent indifference to their vicissitudes and his general aloofness. Of course, Renate was often to experience me as having a similar attitude towards her. Only in his old age, apparently, did his relationship to her begin to change, a shift that was yet again also noticeable in the transference later in her analysis.

As soon as this pseudo-solution fails, Renate's place in the oedipal constellation becomes threatened and insecure: because then she has to compete not only with her mother for her father's love, as all girls do, but also with her sister who, in fantasy, had already secured herself a place made impregnable by her death. The family triangle had by then become a sort of oedipal square, the fourth angle of which was a ghost! By the way, it is remarkable that the only photograph ever taken of Angela was apparently removed from the family album by the father, who later lost it.

In Renate's case, as probably in many other replacement children and in some couples of identical twins, her lifelong search for identity took the form of movements in two opposite directions: further identification with the idealised sister that she was born to substitute, and separation from her. These contradictory movements remind us of the difficulties in normal child development at the separation–individuation phase, with the difference that such a process becomes here a pathological interference with identity formation, instead of being a preparation for it. To provide a feel of the character and configuration of Renate's relationship to her internal objects in this area, I shall confine myself to report without further comments the manifest content of one of her dreams (after nearly three years of analysis).

> I am at the dinner table with my mother and my younger sister. We see the corpse of a young girl lying on the floor near us. My mother and my sister look very frightened, but I am not. The dead girl unexpectedly revives, as if leaving a shell or an armour behind her, and gets up. I invite her to come and sit at the table next to me.

Psychologically speaking Renate had not just one dead sister, but two. There was one whom she was merged with and from whom she had to distance herself and eventually separate; and a second one whom she felt split-off from and whom she longed to reach and integrate within herself. We could perhaps describe this process as the attempted transition towards the establishment of the capacity to experience ambivalence.

Often, a replacement child is given the same name as the one he or she replaces. This was not the case with Renate, but she told me how her parents intended to call her Angela like her sister and only changed their minds about it at the last minute out of superstition: they apparently believed that leaving a nominal difference between the two girls would suffice to make the second one survive whereas the first one had succumbed.[8] This superstition seems to me to emphasise even more the fact that in Renate's parents' minds the two children's identities and their destinies were inseparably intertwined, rather than being evidence of a real wish to differentiate them.

In a case reported by Solemani (1979) the parents gave the name Pierre to the child replacing Peter, who had died of an illness. The mother was convinced that Peter was reborn again in Pierre and that Pierre was therefore "Peter reincarnated". She would even ask Pierre: "You are Peter, aren't you?" Pierre had been conceived as a result of a mistake with contraceptives, soon after Peter had appeared in a dream telling his mother: "Don't cry Mummy, it'll be all right; you'll soon have another boy."

Michelle, another patient of mine, revealed to me about two years after beginning psychotherapy that an older brother, Michael, had died as a toddler when he was still an only child. His parents had tried to replace him with another son but their next child was a girl; a couple of years later they tried again and had another girl. As they did not intend to have more children, they settled for the two girls but, as a compromise, they called the second one Michelle. Michelle came into therapy with a sense of identity confusion ("I am neither Michelle nor Michael," she once stated), schizoid character traits, latent homosexuality, eating problems, and serious difficulties in accepting her female body. She felt unwanted everywhere she went, my consulting room included. "At times", Michelle once told me, "I feel I stink of death, as if Michael's little corpse were glued to me, or stuck inside me". In the course of a dramatic session she remembered being a child and going with her family to Michael's grave. Her mother cried, her father tried to comfort her, she and her sister said that they wanted to have a little brother. Having told me this, Michelle burst into the most desperate sobbing and then confessed that never before had she had a chance to mourn her brother.

On another occasion, Michelle came to her session dressed all in black, which was unusual. "I am convinced that when I was born", she tells me, "my parents, rather than being pleased, went into a state of mourning ... I often feel as if there was a dead foetus inside me; I want to get rid of it, to abort it, but I cannot".

I suggest that the dead foetus inside her doesn't let her feel she is alive. Michelle starts weeping, very quietly. She says her birth was an occasion of grief because she was born the wrong gender. "If only I had died, instead of Michael!" she cries, "He was so marvellous, so perfect!" She remembers how her parents would stare in adoration at their neighbours' child, also called Michael. I comment that perhaps her little brother was so marvellous and perfect precisely because he had died. "Go and tell that to my parents!" she says, with pain and contempt. I say: "I am telling this to you." After a pause she continues: "I know it's all my fault. If only I knew how to repair it ... but it cannot be repaired ... unless I ceased existing myself. There is no other way out." I think to myself that it is precisely because it is not her fault that reparation seems to be such an impossible task.

If, strictly speaking, Michelle cannot be called a replacement child, she does present in many respects a personality structure similar to Renate's, crystallised around a poor self-identity and feelings of unworthiness. In Michelle's case, as well as in Renate's, the interplay of rivalries with the dead siblings and the live ones, and the confusion originating from it, played an important part in their development and relationships.

* * *

Vincent Willem van Gogh was a stillborn baby.

One year later, on the same day in the same month, another Vincent Willem van Gogh was born to the same parents. "We will not be surprised," writes Nagera in his psychoanalytic study of the painter, "at his constant struggle to find an identity for himself in life, an identity in his art belonging only to him, a unique style" (Nagera, 1967, p. 46). Nagera explores in detail the effects of the dead brother's absence/

presence on van Gogh, which he believes haunted the painter all his life. He writes:

> The brother, being stillborn, had never had an identity of his own in reality, but for this very reason an ideal one had been created in the phantasy life of the parents. He would have been the perfect child, the compendium of all virtue, ability and kindness. He would always have done everything right, and especially where Vincent failed, the other, the dead Vincent, would have been successful. This extreme degree of idealization of a dead child … explains the high ego-ideals which he set himself, his dread of failing … and his fear of success … Against such high ego-ideals he would, of course, nearly always fall short.
>
> A further important aspect of these conflicts was the unconscious dread of competing with the idealized dead Vincent. Unconsciously he must have felt that his success was an attack on the memory of the dead one, an attempt to take his place in the affection of the parents. Such fantasies are highly conflictive since … siblings of a dead child feel in some form responsible for their death … Furthermore, it seems possible that under these circumstances Vincent came to associate death and success. To be recognized as good as the brother or better even it was *necessary* to be dead like him. (Nagera, 1967, pp. 162–63)

And eventually, only a few months after the birth of yet another Vincent (his beloved brother Theo's child), van Gogh committed suicide.

Some of the psychological features that Nagera identified in van Gogh seem to be typical of all replacement children, Renate and Michelle included, although the painter's creative capacity to sublimate his own conflicts into immortal art belonged only to him.

Van Gogh's dread of competition, lest he failed or succeeded, resembles Renate's. In her case it emerged most vividly in the transference. She experienced each session as a test or exam in which she was competing with my other patients, who inevitably scored better marks than her for associating more freely, reporting better dreams, telling me more interesting stories … Everything was for her an uphill struggle of which she already knew the negative outcome. In the few areas where she was competent enough to succeed, she would forever be second best.

Renate's not being herself also took the form of not being good enough. She could not contain within herself the good parts, and so she had to deny them, split them off and project them onto others, onto all those objects of both idealisation and hostile rivalry, including myself, who thus became the unconscious representatives of her dead sister. At the same time she was doomed to experience herself as a helpless outsider: at work, at home, on my couch, among friends, and in the world at large, Renate felt she never fully belonged. She felt she had no right to occupy a prominent position anywhere in the world, because such place was already being occupied, in her mother's heart and in her own unconscious mind, by someone else. She once told me of having dreamt that there was another woman with her in my waiting room, and that she felt confused about which of them I would call in for the session.

Predictably, my role in the transference changed several times, so that I became the depressed mother mourning over Angela's death and unable therefore to give Renate enough attention or love, as in the example quoted above; or the emotionally unavailable father to whom she longed in vain to get close; or the dead sister whom she idealised and could not compete with, and loved and hated for being too present and yet too absent in her life—as indeed I was an invisible presence behind the couch. One of the goals in our analytic work was the reintegration into Renate's personality of the split-off aspects of her self, so far projected onto the dead sister and me.

* * *

I hope that the material on child replacement I have presented here provides an illustration of those psychological phenomena of identity distortion—often on the border between normality and pathology—which I have described as being characterised by the feeling of not being oneself.

The splitting in the ego, which is the unconscious mechanism I consider to be the main feature of these experiences, is also present in the replacement child syndrome where it is the fantasy of the dead sibling that is utilised as a part of the ego and invested with projections. This is mostly a dead part of the ego, an aspect of the personality that is unconsciously associated with depression, a sense of failure, passivity, and guilt.

Replacement children are doomed to live permanently with that sense of not being themselves, which in less extreme cases we all occasionally experience as an intrinsic aspect of being ourselves as persons. A whole can exist only when its component parts have opportunities to manifest themselves separately. But for the replacement child the process of integrating and coming to terms with the split-off parts of the ego associated with the dead sibling remains a more arduous and uncertain task.

CHAPTER THREE

# The window and the door

*It is an infantile superstition of the human spirit*
*that virginity would be thought a virtue*
*and not the barrier that separates ignorance from knowledge.*

—Voltaire

As another instance of those conditions which affect one's sense of personal identity, and which are coloured by one's self-experience within temporal and spatial coordinates, I will now focus my psychoanalytically informed attention on the widespread valuing of virginity.

What is virginity? To avoid misunderstandings, frequent whenever the phenomena under observation are as ambiguous, overdetermined, and anxiety-provoking as this, I will define virginity in the most general of terms as *the absence of the experience of genital intercourse*. Such a definition has a number of features. It applies to all individuals, regardless of age, gender, and sexual orientation. It emphasises the primacy of the genital apparatus over other erogenous zones, in so far as it does not take into account other sexual activities, such as oral sex. It classifies a victim of abuse or rape through genital penetration as no longer a virgin. It leaves room to consider both psychological and physical factors (virginity as a state of mind, as well as a physiological feature of the body). Last but not least, by referring to an "absence" it implies that the phenomenon is as such unrepresentable.

This last consideration is a serious one in the context of our current task. It suggests that our words can describe virginity only indirectly, either through its contrast with the *presence* of other related phenomena (for instance, an individual's sexual activities other than genital intercourse, or the person's feelings about virginity, such as desire, fear, guilt, or shame); or, and more emphatically, by representing the very act of genital penetration that puts an end to it. Indeed, as Bernau points out, "much literature on virginity is about its loss: either through rape, unscrupulous seduction, love, marriage or death" (Bernau, 2007a, p. 80). The character-type of the virgin (an individual either unwilling or unable to engage in a sexual relationship) is frequently met not only in literature, but also in theatre and in films of all genres, whether light comedies, intense dramas, or horror. The condition of *loss* referred to here is, in the wide sense of the word, central to much psychoanalytic thinking—from Freud's original ideas expressed in "Mourning and melancholia" (1917e), to current theoretical and clinical developments from John Bowlby's seminal work on attachment, separation, and loss (1969). It is worth pointing out, though, that while we commonly refer to the loss of virginity, there may be an experience of loss also for those who happen, or deliberately decide, to hold on to it—the loss, that is, of the opportunity to belong to the community of adults who can enjoy an active interpersonal sexual life and are able to procreate children.

Contrary to common belief, the discourse about virginity has far from disappeared in the course of the past several decades from our culture, though it has undergone radical transformations. "Virginity's proliferation of meanings and desires ensures its ongoing presence in Western culture. Virginity is never lost" (Bernau, 2007a, p. xv). On the one hand, and in particular with the gradual dissolution of Victorian morality, partly also thanks to psychoanalysis, culminating with the "sexual revolution" of the 1960s, virginity has lost much of that religious high ground of sanctity, purity, and innocence boasted by those who claimed to have remained chaste, at least until their wedding night. We could mention here, incidentally, that the Christian emphasis on Mary's virginity, so prevalent in our popular culture and iconology,[1] is also reflected in a myriad of other mythologies—from the classical Greek legend of the Minotaur demanding a regular supply of "seven youths and seven maidens" from Athens to be devoured by him, to the modern one, much exploited in literature and cinema, of Count Dracula nightly sinking his teeth into the necks of young virgins to satisfy his thirst for fresh blood.

On the other hand, virginity has also attracted the attention of new fundamentalist groups, such as the American pro-chastity organisation Silver Ring Thing, claiming, among other social and spiritual advantages, a healthier mental life for their sexually abstinent adherents. Hundreds of thousands of young people, it claims, wear with pride their symbolic rings, inscribed with Bible verses, on their left-hand third fingers. I understand these rings to be the latter-day, self-imposed, mini versions of medieval chastity belts.

Is the preservation of virginity, we may then ask, to be understood as a form of self-discipline or as the evidence of sexual repression—or even, at least in some instances, of neurotic psychopathology? Is it an expression of individual freedom to be treasured, or a prison from which to escape as soon as possible? In our post-feminist era a girl may well feel that she does own her body, but that still leaves her with the problem of whether that means renouncing her sexual innocence or holding on to it—a personal dilemma which, in the past, tended to be resolved for the individual within the social community to which she belonged, and who shared similar moral values. A girl may experience her genitals as a closed door (at least for the time being) or else as an open window of fulfilling opportunities, as a potential link with the external world or else as an ambivalently experienced barrier to it.

According to Bernau, virginity can be represented "as a radical choice, a reaction against a world in which sex is just another commodity … But virginity can equally be understood as a consumer choice … It may be less fiercely guarded by most than in previous centuries, but losing one's virginity is still perceived as a threshold moment" (Bernau, 2007b, p. 28). This emphasis on "a threshold moment", between childhood innocence and adulthood experience, is of particular importance, as at least some of the anxieties associated to the loss of virginity, for both boys and girls, belong to the ambiguous border territory of bodily sensations, interpersonal relationships, emotional commitments and sexual morality, and might relate to conflictual wishes and fears of engaging for the first time with a new experience.

People are likely to use a combination of psychological mechanisms, in particular denial and rationalisation, to help them deal (or, more accurately, avoid dealing) with the anxieties that the issue of virginity may evoke for them, such as the insecurity they may feel in relation to their bodies, to their sense of identity, and to getting involved in intimate relationships. As to the defensive use of *denial*, we are all prone to unconsciously deny the existence of realities we find physically, psychologically, morally, or socially unacceptable, or even just too unpleasant. So-called "magical thinking" allows us to make disappear (from our perception, sensation, knowledge, or memory) whatever we dislike, and thus pretend it had never existed in the first place. This mechanism, however, can also be used consciously and deliberately in order to deceive others and, in the process, oneself—a far from uncommon situation in relation to virginity.

*Rationalisation*, on the other hand, consists of finding a pseudo-rational explanation for a fact otherwise experienced as intolerable—the way the fox in Aesop's fable describes the grapes he cannot reach as "sour". Examples of denials and rationalisations in relation to virginity are plentiful and I shall only mention here a few.

Some people may explain away their wish to remain chaste, or rather their fear of genital intercourse, in terms of their conscious concerns about sexually transmitted diseases or unwanted pregnancies—a possible but by no means inevitable consequence of becoming sexually active. Alternatively, others may dismiss the ease with which they engage in their first sexual relationship, often at an extremely young age, by attributing the entire responsibility of it to their partner's insistence, or to peer-group pressures, or to excessive drinking, and anyway claiming indifference to its consequences for themselves.

So-called "technical" virgins, corresponding to the *demi-vierges* of some decades ago, would do "everything *but*" in order to maintain their virginal status,[2] while some no-longer chaste girls rewrite their sexual history by buying themselves plastic-surgical "rehymenisation", much as they could purchase themselves a new nose.

Such denials, rationalisations, and other defensive strategies, I suggest, have the function of replacing the more arduous psychological task of coming to terms with deep-rooted preoccupations which, as I will try to show, are mostly unconscious and stemming from the subjects' early relationship to their parents, and more specifically with unresolved oedipal scenarios.

\* \* \*

In recent times, sexuality seems to have lost the privileged place it once occupied in classical psychoanalytic theories and debates. Even in earlier analytic literature, however, the theme of virginity—how it should be defined, how it relates to other aspects of psychosexual development, which unconscious fantasies are associated to it, how its impact on male and female individuals differs—has been largely neglected. This is in contrast with such other disciplines as anthropology, ethnology, sociology, cultural studies, and feminist theory, a review of whose valuable works on this subject is however beyond the scope of this chapter.

Indeed, even Freud's own study on our topic—the last of his three "contributions to the psychology of love", with the suggestive title "The Taboo of Virginity" (1918a)—is, in line with his earlier essays on "Totem and Taboo" (1912c), a mostly anthropological account of virginity as "a logical continuation of the right to exclusive possession of a woman, which forms the essence of monogamy, the extension of this monopoly to cover the past" (Freud, 1918a, p. 193). According to Freud, even for "primitive people" defloration, often performed ritually before the first act of marital intercourse, "is a significant act ... the subject of a taboo—of a prohibition which may be described as religious" (Freud, 1918a, p. 194). Yates (1930), another psychoanalytic author, believes that the woman values her chastity mostly because "she wishes to preserve her virginity for God. And I think", she adds, "that we will have no great difficulty in seeing that God here is largely a father substitute ... The husband in insisting on virginity in his bride is seeking reassurance of his wish that she should not have belonged to his father" (Yates, 1930, p. 173; pp. 182–183). I would add here: nor to *her own* father.

Summarising the anthropological literature on the subject, Freud (1918a) concludes that explanations of the taboo of virginity include an apprehension about anything which, like the first intercourse, is new and uncanny. He suggests that this taboo is an aspect of a wider one that embraces the whole of sexual life: man's fear of women, experienced as dangerous, whereby their defloration would draw their hostility down upon the man responsible for it because of "the pain which defloration causes a virgin" or rather "the narcissistic injury which proceeds from the destruction of an organ" (Freud, 1918a, p. 202). Finally, most early psychoanalysts who have written about virginity point out that defloration, like menstruation, is connected with the idea of a wound and of bleeding, and in turn with castration anxieties and death (Abraham, 1922; Deutsch, 1944–45; Horney, 1933; Yates, 1930).

These texts, however, do little to enlighten us on what should be of central interest to us analysts: the unconscious significance of the first sexual intercourse for young men and women, and the complex psychodynamic interplay of attachments, separations, identifications and projections involved. An exception is Weissman's detailed case history of "neurotic virginity and old maidenhood", a condition he describes as "a psychological state in which sexual intercourse is warded off unconsciously rather than consciously" and characterised by "the inability to finalize a heterosexual object-relationship" (Weissman, 1964, p. 110). This author explains "neurotic virginity" in terms of early psychosexual maturation: "The intense fixation on the oedipal father was devoid of the typical oedipal wishes present in normal development. The father fixation represented an extension of the strong fixation on the preoedipal mother ... and more regressive oral and sadistic wishes for and fears of the mother" (Weissman, 1964, p. 119). Weissman's explanation constitutes an extension and elaboration of the classical psychoanalytic theory according to which prolonged virginity is attributed to an unresolved oedipal conflict as "the little girl remains unconsciously erotically fixated on her father, whom she cannot give up, and thus is unable to extend her affectionate and sexual feelings to another and suitable male" (Weissman, 1964, p. 111). Analogous considerations, of course, are valid *mutatis mutandis* also for "the little boy".

Two other psychoanalytic authors, Holtzman and Kulish, systematically analyse clinical material on the topic of defloration by relating it to such themes as oedipal conflicts, castration anxieties, sadomasochistic fantasies, blood and menstruation, guilt about masturbation, childbirth, etc. In particular, they insist on "the importance and the reality of the hymen as the representation of the entry into adult female genital sexuality. The representation of the hymen is frequently repressed and often suppressed, and serves as an organizing image around which fantasies and conflicts are elaborated" (Holtzman and Kulish, 1996, p. 325).

The hymen surrounding the entrance to a girl's vagina may be experienced by her as a kind of closed door (but all closed doors, of course, are invitations to be opened...)[3]. One could speculate about the complex of fantasies of what, when opened, would come in through this door:

Pleasure? Pain? Disease? Madness? Or, indeed, about the complex of fantasies of what would flow out: Blood? Babies? The infantile part of the self? The virginal vagina could then be conceptualised as a more-or-less safe container of the sexual self, or, in more general terms, as both a link with the external world and as a barrier to it. As the latter, it could operate as a protection or as an obstacle, or more likely as both things at the same time.

In particular, I would suggest that the hymen constitutes for a girl the anatomical representative of a more-or-less severe superego, a kind of guardian of her bodily self, interpersonal relationships, and sexual morality, to be either complied with or rebelled against. Girls may experience a conflict between, on the one hand, a cultural view of virginity as a virtue, and therefore its loss as a sin, constructed on the religious Manichean opposition between celibate Madonnas and nymphomaniac whores, whereby they should hold on to it at least until their wedding night, if not forever. On the other hand, never having experienced a sexual relationship may make them feel like immature children still emotionally dependent on their families, and they may therefore indulge in the illusion that the renunciation of their virginal status would by itself allow them access to the world of adulthood—girls would then be magically transformed overnight into women, and daughters into (potential) mothers.

At the same time, a girl's ambivalence towards sexual innocence is closely linked, as we have seen, to her relationship to her own mother and to unresolved (or only partially resolved) oedipal conflicts. A girl may want to treasure her virginity—as a part of her anatomy, but also as its mental representation—in so far as she experiences it as a precious gift from her mother who, in the daughter's unconscious fantasy, sacrificed her own in order to conceive and give birth. At the opposite extreme, a girl may want to dispense of it at all costs, and as soon as possible, hating it because she may feel her mother only provided her with it out of jealousy, to prevent her from enacting her oedipal desires towards her father—and, later, towards any other man representing him.

Boys, on the other hand, would tend to find themselves in a less conflictual position, partly because in their case the loss of virginity does not in itself have direct physical consequences on their bodies. It could be argued, in this respect, that the presence of the anatomical membrane of the hymen is a psychologically more important difference between men and women than usually recognised. Furthermore, the cultural view of virginity as a virtue has never applied to the same degree to boys as to girls. For pubescent boys, as many anthropological studies have demonstrated, losing virginity is mainly experienced as a straightforward rite of passage from boyhood into adulthood to be performed, depending on the specific culture, ritually or even quite casually. However, boys who have not resolved their oedipal issues may be unable to renounce their virginity, in so far as they may identify every potential sexual partner with their own mother, and engaging in a sexual relationship would therefore be experienced by them as either betrayal or the enactment of an incestuous fantasy. For such young men genital intercourse with a woman is then likely to be replaced by masturbatory, pregenital and preoedipal activities and fantasies, inasmuch as these, being linked to the "polymorphous perversity" of the child, have a regressive quality.

* * *

The temporal dimension plays a role in the discourse about virginity, in so far as there is a crucial time factor in the decision to be made by adolescents and young adults as to when, and how, they should be dealing with this most personal of issues. Both boys and girls may wonder whether they are old enough, or else worry that they are already too old, for giving up their virginal condition. What we are considering here is not the chronological age of the individuals in question, but their subjective age: their own assessment of how old, mature, responsible, and "ready" they feel they are to engage in a physically, if not also emotionally, intimate relationship with another human being. Such an evaluation, being subjective, is liable to appear inadequate to others, sometimes their peers, more often their parents or others belonging to their parents' generation. Occasionally, this assesment may even appear to have a delusional quality, not unlike that of the anorexics' perception of their bodily shape.

There are also, of course, social norms to be taken into account, including formal laws sanctioning when (not to mention where, how, and with whom) sexual activities are allowed. But, as we well know, rules and taboos only need to exist when there is a wish, often repressed, to break them. Their existence would still affect the decision of young people in this respect, both those who will abide by them as they normally would by other rules, and those who will just ignore them, or deliberately rebel against them.

As to the dimension of space, it concerns virginity in so far as genital sexuality involves the penetration of areas of one's own and/ or of other people's bodies—areas, furthermore, invested with considerable emotional significance, whether because they evoke narcissistic pride, or shame and embarrassment, as well as intense physical sensations, ranging from pleasure to pain. In this respect it would be impossible to ignore the effects of both castration and possession anxieties (see Chapter Eight) in the negotiation of any individual's approach to the issue of virginity.

It would be easy to dismiss this issue as old-fashioned and no longer of concern to the young people of our twenty-first century in the Western world, whose attitude to sexual matters in general, and to the meaning of virginity in particular, is so different from that held by their parents and grandparents. Doing so, however, would mean neglecting, instead of addressing, the fears and anxieties of those many young people still struggling with the difficult tasks of finding what, for them, would be the optimal way of relating to others through their sexual bodies. I have referred several times here to virginity as an "issue" rather than as a "problem", because most young people today will not consider it to be one at all. We should not ignore, however, that for many others the decision to engage for the first time in genital intercourse may indeed feel problematic, conflictual, and the source of much emotional pain, mostly experienced in isolation. We owe it to them not to dismiss their suffering.

## CHAPTER FOUR

# Boundaries of timelessness

*Time's the king of men*
*He's both their parent and he is their grave*
*And gives them what he will, not what they crave.*

—William Shakespeare: *Pericles*, 2:2, 45–47

All psychoanalytic relationships—like human life itself, chess games, and most worldly things—have a beginning and an end.

The player might checkmate his opponent, lose, accept a draw, get bored with the game and quit, or kick the board to the floor in a fit of rage. Either or both participants in the analytic encounter might give it up, emigrate abroad, agree to terminate their meetings, or die. And yet, what Freud had to say about the analysis of a single dream—"It is in fact never possible to be sure that a dream has been completely interpreted" (Freud, 1900a, p. 279)—also applies to psychoanalysis as a whole: however far you go, you can go further; however deep, you can go deeper. In this sense, then, psychoanalysis is ultimately interminable, and can only be interrupted; it must be considered as "interminable within a terminable psychoanalytical treatment" (Berenstein, 1987,

p. 30). If we extended this paradoxical statement about the nature of the analytic relationship to other human relationships too, from the one to the primary object onwards, we might gain some further understanding about the causes of much emotional suffering.

\* \* \*

A large number of papers have been published about various aspects of time and psychoanalysis, as well as several books, including those by Sabbadini (Ed.) (1979), Hartocollis (1983), Laget (1995), Green (2000), Perelberg (2008), and Glocer Fiorini and Canestri (Eds.) (2009). Two authors who have explored this subject systematically and offered original perspectives about its significance are Arlow (1984; 1986) and Hartocollis (1972; 1974–1975). In this article I will give a contribution to the studies on time by focusing on the temporal structure of psychoanalysis.

As to the psychoanalytic space (in its concrete meaning), we know that our work takes place within the walls of the analyst's consulting room, where the analyst sits in a chair and the patient usually lies on a couch. Issues that can arise in relation to the analytic space include intrusions into the consulting room from the outside—such as another patient, a noisy bumble-bee, or a voice—and concerns about those transitional areas that surround the therapist's room: its entrance and exit door, the waiting room, the house, the street … The importance, and often the difficulty, of analysing what happens in such grey territories—in the space between the inside and the outside of the consulting room, in the time between a session and what immediately precedes or follows it—cannot be over-emphasised. To know a country, you must become acquainted with its boundaries.

Certainly the perspective and the focus of attention constantly shift, so that, for instance, an analyst might emphasise, in the course of the interpretation of a dream, that one of its elements is a reference to her own country of origin; or she might stress that the dream itself has taken place on the night preceding the patient's birthday. Both the reference to space and that to time may be true and relevant, but the interpretation of that dream will be centred more around one than the other, as a consequence of the patient's associations and the analyst's choice.

However, much as a clear demarcation between inside and outside is not always possible, it is often impossible to differentiate spatial elements from temporal ones. For instance, when we speak about the waiting room, we are referring to the space of a room, but also to the time of waiting. When we try to describe the experience of the analysand walking across the threshold of the consulting room at the end of a session, we are emphasising both where that experience takes place, and when. The fact that the patient is on the way out of the analyst's room is as crucial to the understanding of its meaning as the fact that this happens after the analyst has announced that their session is over. Often, then, the two dimensions of space and time can and must be considered together. Let me give you some brief clinical vignettes as illustration:

> At the end of her last session before a Christmas break, Anna gets up from the couch and, on her way to my door, stumbles and falls down. She swiftly picks herself up and, looking most embarrassed, leaves my room without saying a word about what has just happened. Upon her return after the holiday, I try to relate Anna's fall to her anxiety about separating from me for the Christmas break. Falling down in my room was her way of letting me know that she wanted to stay there for the following two weeks too, that she needed my help, that she wished me to have some physical contact with her, and so on. The spatial and temporal dimensions could not be isolated one from the other: had Anna fallen down on the same day in her bathroom, or in the same place at a different time in her analysis, the meaning of that accident, and my understanding and interpretation of it, would have been different.

> On leaving my consulting room for the last time after eight years of therapy, Brian closed the door behind his back. He had never done that before, not even once. I believe that Brian had shut my door as an unconscious enactment of the fantasy of locking me into my consulting room forever. In there, where he was not allowing himself to come anymore to see me, no one else would have been able to reach me either, and I would have been imprisoned in solitary confinement for a timeless eternity.

> For Kate analysis was, in her experience, an uninterrupted piece of music that could not tolerate breaks in its performance, or composition, without coming to a premature end. The real breaks that exist in it—the transitional space between waiting and consulting room, between the door and the couch and the door again—like the intervals between feeds in the experience of the baby, undergo

magical denial: timelessness is allowed to have no boundaries. "I am in hell," Kate once told me, "I come here, then you tell me it is time to stop, then it is hell again". Between *here* and *hell*—between timelessness and time—there is no intermediate region.

This brings me closer to what I consider to be a central aspect in the temporal dimension of psychoanalysis: the peculiar admixture of strict adherence to the precise, though hopefully not obsessionally enforced, rules about time in the analytic setting on the one hand; and on the other, the indeterminate, timeless atmosphere of the analytic encounter itself. This atmosphere "is created by a deliberately relaxed unconcern with the passage of time and by a calculated seeming disregard for the duration of the treatment" (Namnum, 1972).

The formal time boundaries in psychoanalysis are normally set and controlled by the analyst, who—being in charge of deciding upon the duration of sessions and the dates of holidays, and of announcing the beginning and the end of each meeting—can be seen as the true "master of time". At this level at least, the analytic relationship follows the pace dictated by the analyst's clock and by his calendar.

H. D. (Hilda Doolittle), in her account of her analysis with Freud, describes how he saw himself as having responsibility for time within the session: "The other day the Professor had reproached me for jerking out my arm and looking at my watch. He had said, 'I keep an eye on the time. I will tell you when the session is over. You need not keep looking at the time, as if you were in a hurry to get away'" (H. D., 1956, p. 17).

* * *

The above issues will be further illustrated by the following analytic material:

> When Daniel left his session, he believed I had deprived him of three minutes of his time; he was furious with me and felt that I was exploiting him. On his way home, though, he realised that in fact I had kept him for fifty-two minutes, instead of the usual fifty. He would not have been caught unprepared by my announcing him the end of the session, had he calculated the time correctly during it; he could have decided to stop talking at the right time, as he always does, thus being in control of terminating the session himself and not having to feel rejected by me. Daniel arrived to the

next session without wearing his wristwatch. He explained that, as an experiment, he had left it outside in the waiting room, in his coat pocket. But now, without it, he felt very anxious as he had to rely entirely upon me. Later in the session Daniel suddenly felt like turning around, grabbing my arm and looking at my watch; not to know the time, he said, was almost unbearable for him, be it in his kitchen, in the street or in my consulting room.

About half an hour into this session, he reported a dream from the previous night. While telling me this dream, Daniel became overwhelmed with anxiety and asked me whether there was enough time left for him to continue with it. The dream was as follows:

> I am in Barbara's car; she is driving and I am not wearing the safety seatbelt. I am frightened that we might have an accident and get hurt, or that the police might stop us and punish me with imprisonment for an indefinite term. I feel entirely in Barbara's hands. She is now trying to park the car, and there is a lorry coming towards us. I wake up in a state of fear.

His associations link the car seatbelt to his wristwatch: not wearing either is dangerous. I am Barbara, in whose hands he has unwittingly placed himself, thus becoming exposed to danger and being made vulnerable. The lorry is the overwhelming anxiety that could catch up with him and destroy him, finding him unprepared to cope. The police represent his internal persecutor, both his rigid father and myself in the transference, punishing him for his unacceptable wishes by keeping him indefinitely in prison: an indefinitely long (or short) session with me.

One of the meanings of Daniel's relationship to time became evident a few months later, when he described how his mother perceived him as growing thinner every time she saw him. Before he leaves her to go back home she always provides him with chocolate bars and crisps, which he experiences ambivalently, as both a caring gesture and a way of infantilising him. Having told me this, he then felt silent. When I asked him what he was thinking about, Daniel replied that he wanted me to take over in these last minutes of the session, to feed him with nice analytic food so that I would remove from him the anxiety of starving himself with silence. At that moment he felt that he could not be an independent adult capable of looking after himself properly without growing too thin, because suddenly, at the end of the fifty-minute-long analytic meal, he would be asked to leave the table. Underlying this anxiety, Daniel also expressed the fear that if he started talking, he would become unable to stop; he would be going over time and be swamped by greed and eventually guilt. My taking over with my words would then have relieved him of the anxiety pertaining to both sides of the oral coin: starvation and greed.

By the way, Daniel has never worn a watch again in a session. His internal clock tells him more or less when his time is coming to the end, which means that, not unlike before, he still remains quiet for the last three or four minutes of each session.

* * *

Antinucci-Mark, following in McDougall's (1982) footsteps, compares the analytic scenario to what happens in the theatre:

> The opening of the door is analogous to raising the curtains which reveal the theatre, its boundaries and its contents … What we define as the theatrical event is rigidly delimited by the duration of the performance and the space of the stage. The phenomenon which occurs in the consulting room has strict temporal boundaries and follows quite closely the concept of unity of time, place and action which classical theory borrowed from Aristotle's poetic conceptions. Precisely because of these fixed norms a multiplicity of experiences can be represented. (Antinucci-Mark, 1986, p. 15)

The timeless quality of the content of analysis is determined by, and in constant interaction with, such formal time arrangements, set by the analyst and altered only under exceptional circumstances. It is this *contrast of temporalities* that shapes the analytic encounter, modulating its rhythm and punctuating its discourse. Each of these temporalities is unthinkable without the other. Their paradoxical coexistence can be exemplified by the fairytale of *The Sleeping Beauty*: the universe of time-lessness, of the frozen breath, of the eternal indistinctness between life and death, can only emerge from the background of nature and reality, of movement and "normal" time surrounding the boundaries of the spellbound castle. What is most interesting to us is not one world or the other, but the fine edge separating them: the kiss of the handsome prince, the first smile of our beauty awakening to sexuality (Bettelheim,

1976, p. 225), the initial effort of the clocks of time to start moving again after their rusty centennial paralysis.

Within the safe temporality of the fifty minutes, of the five weekly sessions, of the consistency, continuity and repetitiveness of the analytic process and its rituals, regression to a more primitive timelessness is facilitated. Unstructured representations related to primary process logic and to unconscious functioning can thus emerge. These take the shape of free associations, where the "freedom" we require (and never fully obtain) from our patients is mostly freedom from the exacting bonds of time.

It is because of the coexistence of different temporalities that we can come across those rare but exciting moments of insight and enlightenment in the course of the psychoanalytic process. Some of the most intense moments in our existence—giving birth to a baby, falling in love, the heights of sexual, mystical or aesthetic pleasure, probably the transition to death itself—share with the analytic experience features of its specific temporality, including the sense of timelessness. Their main phenomenological features are a partial loss of the sense of identity, an "oceanic" fusion with the object, and a momentary slackening of the bonds of time involving a regression to a more primitive temporality.

* * *

As already mentioned in Chapter One, Freud had pointed out that the temporal laws that govern our relationship with the external world do not operate in the unconscious: "The processes of the system Ucs.", he wrote, "are timeless; *i.e.,* they are not ordered temporally, are not altered by the passage of time; they have no reference to time at all" (Freud, 1915e, p. 187).

Evidence of the timelessness of the unconscious can be found not only in the structure of dreams and in their manifest content, but also in the still undifferentiated experience of time in early infancy, when the instinctual need and its gratification form a magically inseparable unit. As I have tried to show, originally time is not yet organised around a three-dimensional structure, but is experienced instead as omnipresent— a condition that I have described as an eternal present that transcends the boundaries of time. It is related on the one hand to the pleasure principle and to primary narcissistic omnipotence, whereby needs and wishes are magically satisfied without delay, before the establishment of a past dimension (memory) and a future one (expectation); and on the other hand, to a lack of clear differentiation of the self from the outside world, before the establishment of object and self constancy, of whole object-relationships, and of the sense of identity.

The spatiotemporal components of the analytic setting have for the patient a structuring function similar, in many respects, to the supportive (holding, containing, facilitating) environment provided to the growing child by good-enough parenting. In fact, the experience of time during psychoanalysis is often not intrinsically different from that of the young child. The analytic regression manifests itself also and most specifically in this respect. The weakening of the ego defences and of secondary process functioning, facilitated by the structure itself of the analytic setting, and in particular by its temporal arrangements, gives way not only to a freer expression of unconscious material, but also to a more primitive experience of time and relationship to it. The analyst, in a state of freefloating attention, has to accomplish the "impossible" task of loosening control over his ego in order to listen to the analysand's internal world, while preserving the capacity for secondary process activities in order to reflect upon this internal world, understand it and interpret it; he has to read the words of a text, while at the same time reading between its lines; he has to listen with his "third ear" (see Reik, 1948) while also listening with the other two.

Within safe analytic boundaries the temporal sequence of events becomes to a large extent irrelevant, the chrono/logic of everyday life gives way to a different timeless reality. What belongs to the past is fused with the *hic et nunc* of the transference; memories of old gratifications and frustrations get mixed up with wishes and fears of future ones; the fifty minutes of a session can seem to last a brief minute or an eternity; a dreamlike atmosphere can pervade the analytic space and time; a rigid sense of identity and clear-cut demarcation in the relationship between the two participants in the process, facilitated by the paradoxical predicament of the patient on the couch who is at the same time talking to herself and to her analyst, gives way to a more regressed state of undifferentiation between self and object. Within this temporality sessions unfold according to unevenly rhythmical patterns—of utterances and silences, monologues and dialogues, sighs, pauses and encouraging noises, associations, reconstructions, and interpretations—that bear little resemblance to the time structures of the normal extra-analytical interactions among adults.

This, of course, only applies to some patients and for brief periods of time; analysands often resist relinquishing their hold over their more habitual temporality, unconsciously fearing that a regressive attitude to time would lead to loss of ego-identity and to an excessive dependence upon their analyst.

> Eleanor was usually withdrawn and detached from me in her sessions, as indeed she found it most difficult to express any warmth towards her mother for whom she had mostly ambivalent feelings. But occasionally she would indulge in the fantasy of meeting me outside the consulting room in order to go for romantic walks in the woods, or of soon terminating her analysis so that there would be no more formal obstacles to us getting married. In my interpretations, I tried to bring Eleanor's fantasies back (spatially and temporally) to the here-and-now of the transference. I suggested that her wish to have a closer relationship with me, which she had safely moved outside and after her analysis, was in fact a displaced and dis-timed wish to have such an intimacy with me inside my consulting room and in the present.

When patients allow themselves to experience in their analysis the more timeless reality I have referred to above, this has to be understood and interpreted in the context of the transference. Its main psychodynamic mechanisms are regression and repetition, both of which are characterised by a temporal component: regression inasmuch as the transference involves the abandonment of the current mental organisation and a restructuring of the internal world according to previous and only partially overcome ways of functioning and object-relating; repetition in so far as it draws its power from unresolved conflicts, forgotten traumata, and repressed memories, rooted in the past. Thus, in the here-and-now of the transference, childhood experiences, family romances and scenarios, screen and traumatic events, and whole object-relations patterns are sometimes reactivated and actualised with the same emotional qualities and intensity as their original models.

The transference, in its relation to time, emerges then as the theatre of a paradoxical situation: within it, and through it, we analyse the past in order to give meaning to the present, and at the same time we interpret the present in order to recover the past. Remembering is a creative activity that takes place in the present, and that through the process of *après-coup* (see Birksted-Breen, 2003) inevitably distorts the past. The "essence [of the psychoanalytic process] is the constant and repeated interaction of past with present and present with past, activating each other, as if, in effect, time was transcended" (Namnum, 1972, p. 740). The transference with all its past reverberations and echoes is still a new relationship.

But psychoanalysis does not simply consist of an interplay between the past and present temporal dimensions. Inasmuch as its two participants embark upon it in the hope of bringing about new life rather than digging out old corpses, of bringing about some change in the organisation of the internal world of one of them (though sometimes they have to accept the impossibility of it) the psychoanalytic experience is an endeavour fundamentally projected towards the future. Without this dimension, creative timelessness would turn into sterile repetitiveness and analysis would get embedded into the meaningless impasse that is so typical of patients with conditions characterised by autistic, "disaffective" or borderline connotations (see Innes-Smith, 1987).

* * *

I have so far referred to the whole therapeutic process of psychoanalysis, and to each single psychoanalytic session. It is interesting to note how the temporal structure of the latter reflects and repeats that of the former, and is in turn reflected and repeated in it.

> Francis, a middle-aged patient, always arrived obsessionally on time for his sessions. As a result of some analytic work, we discovered his punctuality to be a defensive reaction formation against coming to terms with his sense of hopelessness for having arrived to psychoanalysis too late in his life.

Without stretching the similarities too far, it might be useful to compare the first session of a long analysis (where some of the main themes may be first introduced) with the opening of each single session, often suggestive of the atmosphere of the rest of the session itself. Like the listener of the overture of an opera, the analyst is faced with a sort of initial concentration or recapitulation of themes which will then be referred to, repeated, developed, and worked through in the course of the following forty or so minutes, and of the following weeks, months or years.

Furthermore, the passage from the "real" time in the outside world to the timeless atmosphere of analysis, and then back to a time-bound external reality, again applies both to analysis as a whole and to each individual session. Some analysts might prepare their patients for termination by gradually introducing elements of reality into the relationship and replacing some of their original transference interpretations with more reality-oriented ones. Analogously, most analysts tend not to leave their patients with an excessive amount of unworked-through anxiety between their meetings, by trying to avoid deeper interpretations in the last few minutes of each session, or in the last session before a weekend or a holiday.

The integrity of the ego functions, allowing the patient to move in and out of regressive states (in and out of the session) is an important condition for analysability.

As Greenson writes:

> In order to approximate free association, the patient must be able to regress in his thinking, to let things come up passively, to give up control of his thoughts and feelings, and to partially renounce his reality testing. Yet we also expect the patient to understand us when we communicate to him, to do some analytic work on his own, to control his actions and feelings after the hour, and to be in contact with reality ... [We] require the patient to possess the capacity to regress and rebound from it. (Greenson, 1967, p. 54)

I remember a rule-of-thumb I was taught in art classes many years ago: the darkest and the lightest areas of shading should never be at the edges of a drawing. Something similar would apply to the "edges" of psychoanalysis and analytic sessions alike, to their beginnings and their ends. Here the so-called "tact" of the analyst, the timing of her interpretations, her awareness of how the analysand will experience them and be capable of tolerating the resulting anxiety, are all issues of technical importance.

Returning now to the somewhat rhetorical question asked earlier in this chapter, about whether psychoanalysis is *endliche* or *unendliche*, terminable or interminable, I would like to dodge it by answering that it is always lengthy. Analyst and patient alike commit themselves to share the same space for a regular and limited period of time—say fifty minutes a day, five days a week—over an unlimited number of years. As we will see in the next chapter, such a commitment, and what derives from it, lies at the core of the psychoanalytic process.

## CHAPTER FIVE

# Open-endedness and termination

*When the Wayfarer asked how long a journey lay ahead,*
*the Philosopher merely answered "Walk!"*
*and afterwards explained his apparently unhelpful reply*
*on the ground that he must know the length of the Wayfarer's stride*
*before he could tell how long his journey would take ...*
*In point of fact, the question as to the probable duration*
*of a treatment is almost unanswerable.*

—Sigmund Freud: On beginning the treatment, 1913
*Standard Edition, 12*, p. 128

Freud famously compared analysis to "the noble game of chess" (1913c, p. 123), but only described its opening moves, not the final ones. Yet, we know these to be crucial to the outcome of both psychoanalysis and chess.

\* \* \*

Certain events, experiences, and relationships are fixed in duration, and consequently their length is predictable. We know that our babies are likely to be born about nine months after conception and that a psychoanalytic session lasts fifty minutes (at least in Great Britain). We know that a summer love affair is likely to be over at the end of the holiday, or that the chess battle is reaching its conclusion when the white king is surrounded by black pieces checking him all around the board.

Other events, experiences, and relationships, most of them perhaps, are more open in time and their conclusions are to a large extent unpredictable. A young child does not know when his absent mother is likely to come back, if at all. A major source of distress during wartime is not knowing when the war is going to finish. We might ignore how long an illness is going to last, or when an analysis or a chess game are going to end. Even if we have the conscious knowledge that we are going to die, we do not know when. And, of course, we adopt all available psychological defence mechanisms, such as denial and rationalisation, to deal with the anxieties that such uncertainties arouse in us: a new drug will make me promptly recover; the war will be over by Christmas.

Great artists, as Freud himself conceded, have the deepest understanding of the human mind.

> 'Three days and nights of awful suffering and then death. Why, it might happen to me, all of a sudden, at any moment,' he thought, and for an instant he was terrified. But immediately, he could not have explained how, there came to his support the old reflection that this thing had befallen Ivan Ilyich and not him, and that it ought not and could not happen to him … After which reflection Piotr Ivanovich cheered up and began to ask with interest about the details of Ivan Ilyich's end, as though death were some mischance to which only Ivan Ilyich was liable, but he himself was not. (Tolstoy, 1886, pp. 107–108)

My schematic differentiation of experiences according to their temporal predictability is valuable in so far as our knowledge, or lack thereof, about the termination of a given event or relationship deeply affects how we perceive it. Our appreciation of the psychoanalytic relationship would be quite different if we were to know how much of it was still left to take place. Indeed, after a decision about termination has been reached, analysis becomes different to what it was before. In the rare occasions when a human being knows when he is going to die— the case of a man sentenced to death by a court of law or by a terminal illness with a predictable course—our experience of life, our attitude towards ourselves and others, our priorities and values and beliefs, inevitably undergo dramatic changes.

Whatever structural similarities one may identify, a crucial feature in the psychoanalytic encounter remains the difference between the temporal dimension of each individual session (known, regular, predictable) and that of the analytic relationship as a whole (unknown, varying, unpredictable) provided that the condition of its open-endedness is being respected. If our technique is such that it does not aim towards the preservation of this vitally important contrast of temporalities, the essence and spirit of the analytic process itself undergo major alterations.

Such a contrast of temporalities can be upset in at least two different ways. The first one, devised by Lacan and supported by his followers, consists of the explicit introduction in the analytic contract of a rule according to which the therapist can arbitrarily decide to cut a session short if he feels that not much is to be achieved by letting it continue for the normal fifty minutes. This technique may be informed by a well-intentioned goal to punctuate the patient's discourse, or to disrupt her assumptions about the analytic setting as something static and unchangeable; and perhaps some patients might be stimulated to work harder (whatever that means) by the fear of having their sessions suddenly curtailed. However, I remain opposed to such a distortion of the analytic atmosphere and to what patients could so easily experience as a persecutory manipulation of their freedom.

The second way in which we can disturb the contrast of analytic temporalities is by imposing an artificial date for termination of psychoanalysis. This can be the result either of a particular choice of treatment, such as brief or focal therapy or crisis intervention; or of pressures from external circumstances; or of the analyst's conscious decision to put an ultimatum to a patient in order, for instance, to achieve quicker results. We are all familiar with the oft-repeated objection to psychoanalysis as being too lengthy a form of treatment. Freud described the wish to shorten analytic treatment as "justifiable", but he added that "unfortunately, it is opposed by ... the slowness with which deep-going changes in the mind are accomplished—in the long resort, no doubt, the 'timelessness' of our unconscious processes" (Freud, 1913c, p. 130). There are still no shortcuts available, much as there is generally no easy route to check-mating a masterful opponent in chess.

*  *  *

Commonly associated with the premature end of pregnancies, the English word "termination" is misleading when used in relation to the ending of analysis, especially in so far as such an ending should be the result of a carefully considered decision rather than an unfortunate accident. Nevertheless, the word termination has entered psychoanalytic language, and indeed there already exists a vast literature on it, which includes Schachter (1992), Orgel (2000), Ferraro and Garella (2001), Bonovitz (2007), Gabbard (2009) and Sirois (2011), to name a few. Rather than attempting to review it here, I shall focus on what I consider to be the fundamental and distinctive feature of psychoanalysis concerning its duration: its open-endedness. This aspect of our clinical work is rarely written about, yet I think it is at least as important as the consistency of the setting, the reclining position of the patient on the couch (see Chapter Seven), or the frequency of sessions (a currently much debated issue in the context of different models of training).

\* \* \*

What I call the open-ended nature of psychoanalysis (which also applies, by the way, to other relationships, such as friendships) does not concern its terminability, nor what may happen after its end but, quite on the contrary, what happens at its outset. Open-endedness is about the freedom that psychoanalyst and patient have to start the analysis without being under pressure to decide when to bring it to a close. While some patients, or indeed analysts, may become anxious when faced with such an indefinitely long span of time opening up like an abyss in front of them, other "wayfarers" will instead feel reassured by the opportunity to embark on their analytic journey without feeling rushed to conclude it. It is as if analyst and patient were to say to each other: "Yes, it will end one day, but we do not know when, nor do we need to make any plans about it yet. We trust that it will end in due course, when we feel ready for it."

To believe, as I do, that psychoanalysis is by definition an open-ended relationship is not to say that analyst and patient should go on meeting forever. This, in turn, does not rule out that analysis could be considered as interminable. Let me clarify: analyst and patient at some point decide on, and then stick to, a date on which to stop their regular sessions. Coinciding with the interval of time—usually several months—between this decision being reached and the agreed day for the last session, this terminal phase forms an essential part of the analytic process. It gives both analyst and analysand a chance to face and work through issues of separation, loss and mourning, and more specifically to come to terms with the reality of having to leave behind what is inevitably an "unfinished business". This process should also help both parties to accept that psychological problems, and more generally existential dilemmas, cannot be resolved once and for all, and that it is an illusion to believe that analysis could protect us from all future difficulties, and ultimately from death.

The objective fact that at some point sessions, and life, come to an end, only apparently contradicts the fact that a successfully concluded analysis is by its definition *interminable* (Freud, 1937c); it has to involve the internalisation of the analyst as a good (or rather, good-enough) object, and therefore its continuous survival in the mind of the analysand long after the last session has taken place. In other words, the analytic sessions end, but the analytic process continues. It is my experience that some patients resist internalising the analyst precisely because they are afraid that this will bring their analysis closer to its conclusion—a paradoxical condition involving the unconscious need to remain independent from the analysis in order to stay dependent on it.

* * *

"I have made it my habit, when I know little about a patient, only to take him on at first provisionally, for a period of one or two weeks … a *sounding* in order to get to know the case and to decide whether it is a suitable one for psycho-analysis" (Freud, 1913c, pp. 123–124). While a thorough diagnostic assessment of prospective patients, occasionally requiring more than one consultation, is of essential importance for making a referral, Freud's recommendation for such a "sounding" before embarking on a full analysis has mostly gone out of fashion. I believe this is so because the trial period, being by definition the opposite of an open-ended situation, would not be a true reflection of the experience of being in psychoanalysis, and therefore could not be used to provide any clear indication as to how the analysis proper would then develop. (Test-driving a Ford would not be of much help in deciding whether or not to buy a Jaguar!)

This practice, however, has not entirely disappeared. A psychotherapist I had in supervision worked in a consultation centre where clinicians were expected to see patients for a four-to-six-week assessment period before deciding whether to then offer open-ended therapy. My supervisee once reported that one of his patients, who after much hesitation had become engaged to get married, arrived to one of those "trial period" sessions in a state of panic, announcing she had lost her engagement ring. When she realised she could have left it in the therapist's bathroom, where she had just been before her session and where she had removed it to wash her hands, she rushed out of the consulting room and went back to the bathroom where, much to her relief, she found her ring. The therapist interpreted the patient's ambivalence about her relationship with her boyfriend, about being engaged to him, and about the prospect of getting married. I suggested that, alongside such anxieties, the patient was also expressing through her parapraxis her ambivalence about getting "engaged" for a trial period to the therapist, and about the prospect of getting "married" to him for an open-ended therapy.

*  *  *

Perhaps the open-endedness of psychoanalysis is only rarely discussed because it is almost taken for granted; however, this should not be the case. Late in his life, Freud became critical of his own earlier attempts to speed up, or to close down, the analysis of some of his patients, including the Wolf Man, by artificially imposing a date for termination. "This blackmailing device", he wrote in no ambiguous terms, "cannot guarantee to accomplish the task completely. On the contrary, we may be sure that, while part of the material will become accessible under the pressure of the threat, another part will be kept back and thus become buried, as it were, and lost to our therapeutic efforts" (Freud, 1937c, p. 218).

Other times, it is from its very beginning that analysis is set up as a not open-ended process, for instance, when a new patient knows that he is only going to remain in the country for a few months, or whenever the duration of the analysis is determined by the funds made available by the national health system or through private insurance. I have come across another instance of this kind of situation, having supervised analytically oriented psychotherapy students whose training cases were referred to them on condition that they should continue for, say, at least two years. Although setting only the minimum and not the maximum duration of the therapy, in my experience such an instruction, or injunction, always interferes with the analytic work, the stated period often becoming a focus of much enactment through premature interruptions—with "obedient" and obsessional patients stopping exactly after two years; "rebellious" ones aborting it a few weeks before the stipulated time; paranoid ones convinced that they would be thrown out after the two-year deadline; and others correctly understanding, and often bitterly resenting, that the time condition was intended for the benefit of their therapists (required to see them for at least two years in order to qualify) rather than for their own.

Similar limitations on the duration of analysis apply also to cases seen under various schemes in many psychoanalytic institutions (including my own British Psychoanalytical Society) whenever funds are made available to analysands to cover their fees for, say, up to 500 sessions. While understanding the financial rationale behind these limitations, I would question whether analyses embarked upon under such conditions can be considered to be true analyses at all. This, of course, is not to deny their potential therapeutic value, nor that of other "brief" or otherwise time-limited forms of psychotherapy, but to emphasise what I consider a crucial difference between psychoanalysis and other kinds of intervention.

The reasons for the centrality of the experience of psychoanalysis as an open-ended endeavour are complex, but ultimately always associated to the timelessness of primary process functioning in our unconscious life. Unconscious timelessness, in turn, also relates to the infantile experience of time which I have described in Chapter One as omnipresent: a narcissistic time where the modalities of past, present, and future are still largely undifferentiated, much as the self is still largely undifferentiated from the external world. Open-endedness establishes and represents a dialectically creative tension between our contrasting needs for preconscious control of time and unconscious, timeless freedom. Such tension is reproduced in the structure itself of psychoanalysis: I am referring here to its ever-present contrast of temporalities between, on the one hand, the sense of timelessness often characterising the experience of being in analysis and, on the other, the rigorous temporal structure of the psychoanalytic setting, with its hours always fifty minutes long, its codified number of weekly meetings, its regular holiday breaks, and its general consistency of time arrangements (see Chapter Three).

The open-endedness of psychoanalysis is such an important feature because this is also a characteristic of our closest family relationships: with our parents, around whom transference is constructed; with our marital partners (at least, for those who believe in the indissoluble nature of marriage: "til death do us part"); and with our children—in other words, all of the most significant relationships in our lives. One doesn't normally expect these relationships to come to an end before death (though sometimes they do)—and, if one also happened to believe in an afterlife, one could even be convinced they will continue for eternity.

Strictly speaking, of course, none of this applies to the psychoanalytic relationship, which we do know should, and will, eventually come to an end, even when we may delude ourselves that it will not. As I have said, what really matters, is that the psychoanalytic process can, and should, begin as open-ended, and then continue until a time when both analyst and analysand believe they are ready to separate. However, we must be aware that the eventually inevitable step of deciding on a day for termination radically transforms the nature of the psychoanalytic relationship. It alters the analyst's and the analysand's experience of time within the analysis by turning it into a finite journey, by creating perhaps a sense of anxiety ("We'd better hurry! Time is running out.") or of relief ("At long last, after all this hard work, we see the light at the end of the tunnel.") and it challenges those unconscious fantasies of interminability, of regressive fusion, of never-ending dependency, of timelessness, and of immortality that characterised it while it was still open-ended. Once the powerful, specific focus on the last session is introduced into the material, associations can no longer be free (by which I mean that they are likely to become even less free than they were before). In a sense, then, we could paradoxically state that analysis ends not with the last session, but on the day that analyst and analysand agree on when their last session will occur. A parallel could be drawn here with the way in which a person's very experience of being alive is transformed after he has been condemned to know the date of his death by the sentence of a judge or by the prognosis of a physician.

Sometimes a premature termination is forced upon the analytic couple by such factors as inadequate assessment and referral, the patient's negative therapeutic reaction, or the analyst's technical incompetence. Other times it is imposed by external circumstances, such as major changes in financial conditions, the patient's or the analyst's serious illness, death, relocation to a different city, the analyst retiring from work, etc.

> My patient Ginette is unable to end her analysis, but she feels she must "take a break" (allegedly for financial reasons) in the hope to come back at a later time. Her ambivalence about making a

decision is tangible. Suddenly, she changes the subject and starts talking about a cousin who had committed suicide a few years previously (this material was already presented several times in the past and was always charged with considerable anxiety). I suggest to Ginette that she feels that perhaps her plans to leave analysis prematurely have suicidal overtones … She bursts into tears.

It must be noticed that even when analyst and analysand can make a joint decision unencumbered by these extraneous factors about when to end, such a decision—apparently reached on the rational grounds of objective clinical assessment—is in fact often arbitrary. Of course there are always good reasons behind it, motivated by whatever theoretical model the analyst may have adopted: the symptoms have disappeared (a necessary but not sufficient condition); the patient's ego has been strengthened; the transference, or transference neurosis, has been resolved; the analysand's personality has undergone major structural modifications; the superego is now less inflexible and more benign; "common unhappiness" has replaced "hysterical misery" (Freud, 1893b, p. 305). But, with perhaps a few exceptions, I think no one can honestly say whether, towards the end of a lengthy analytic journey, a patient could not have as easily stopped it a few weeks earlier, or would not have gained some benefit from continuing it for a few more months.

* * *

Long before a date for termination can be agreed upon, a number of narcissistic, regressive, or catastrophic fantasies about ending are likely to emerge. These can be subsumed under two major categories. To the first belong fantasies about one's analysis going on forever, as if the hard realities of separation and loss could be magically denied. Such fantasies are related to our omnipotent wish for, and belief in, immortality, in turn deriving from the timelessness of our unconscious life and the "omnipresent" experience of time in the infant to which I have made reference above. The second group of fantasies, in contrast to the first ones but not necessarily incompatible with them and often to be found alongside them, centres around the mostly unrealistic fear that one's analysis could be suddenly and traumatically interrupted (and here the word "terminated", or rather "aborted", would indeed be appropriate), before a time when the conditions for bringing it to a satisfactory conclusion could be established. I believe these two complementary fantasies, which always require careful interpretation, are present in all analyses, though of course their relative importance, forms of manifestation, and relation to past emotional history vary from patient to patient. Creating the opportunity to explore and understand them is an important aspect of our clinical work, and an indispensable condition before a date for termination can be considered (De Simone, 1994).

* * *

Different metaphors are often advanced in psychoanalytic literature, as well as from the couch, to represent the experience of termination. These are often valid, at least for some analysands, but like all other theoretical models they fail to convey the experience in its full complexity, only highlighting selected aspects of it. Some authors, for instance, describe termination as a kind of birth (or rebirth)—a time when the patient's new self is ready to emerge after the lengthy gestational dependence on a maternal analysis. Others describe the stage of termination as a gradual process comparable to the weaning of an infant from the breast; these analysts sometimes also advocate the technique of "weaning" their patients from their dependency on analysis through the gradual reduction in the frequency of sessions, here being compared to feeds, as a way of reducing the intensity of the process in preparation for the final separation. I am not myself in favour of such practice, on the grounds that I believe that if patients are ready they should end, and if they are not they should continue; otherwise, what is actually ended, with all the emotions pertaining to the loss, is not the experience of analysis, but a diluted, and therefore different, version of it. The analysis itself has *de facto* been interrupted and left unfinished. (Nor, for similar reasons, am I in favour of ending analyses at a time of the year to coincide with a holiday, *i.e.* just before Christmas or a long summer break.)

Another common way of describing the process of analytic termination is to compare it with the stages of attachment, separation, and individuation—those developmental phases studied through the observation of babies and of toddlers, and later repeated, *mutatis mutandis*, in adolescence. Finally, and more dramatically, termination is often associated with death itself, with an emotional point of no return. Introducing the controversial concept of the presence of a death drive beyond the pleasure principle, Freud suggested that human beings, in fact all living beings, are regressively pulled back towards the deadness of inorganic matter. If "everything living dies for internal reasons—becomes inorganic once again—then we shall be compelled to say that *the aim of all life is death*" (Freud, 1920g, p. 38). This "far-fetched speculation", as Freud himself describes it (Freud, 1920g, p. 24), perhaps more appealing as a poetic metaphor than as a scientifically demonstrable fact, could be extended to the course of analysis itself.

Even without sharing the rather extreme assertion that "ending is what psychotherapy is all about" (Schlesinger, 2005, p. xi), we could state, in a nutshell, that as for life (and for love, and friendship, and the noble game of chess), the end of analysis is already present in its beginning, that paradoxically, the termination of an open-ended analysis is already there in its first session. I would add that those analysts and analysands who find it difficult to resolve dependency issues and to bring an open-ended analysis to its conclusion, arbitrary as its timing may be, are often individuals who also in their personal lives have problems letting go of their objects, losing them and separating from them—for instance, parents who struggle to let their adolescent children grow independent of them. I consider such character difficulty as stemming from inadequate, idealising, or excessively ambivalent pre-oedipal or oedipal attachments, for the capacity to give up our objects after an appropriate amount of mourning is a sign that the relationship we had established with them was a truly mature one.

> My patient Bruna, in analysis five times a week for several years but beginning to consider termination, once told me: "You must be in despair at the thought that you could never get rid of me." My first thought was to understand her statement as an instance of projection, and that what she really meant was: "You must be in despair at the thought that *I* could never get rid of *you*." But I interpreted instead the aggressive quality of the expression "to get rid of" and queried: "*Getting rid of* rather than properly ending?" She replied: "Nothing ever properly ended in my life."

When searching for a suitable way to end these reflections on such an open-ended topic as the open-endedness of psychoanalysis, I came across the words of Constantine P. Cavafy (1911). Echoing Robert Louis Stevenson's "To travel hopefully is a better thing than to arrive" (1881), the Greek poet warns us that what really matters is not to reach the final destination, but to prolong and enjoy the journey towards it, the experience of the voyage itself.

> As you set out for Ithaka,
> hope the voyage is a long one,
> full of adventure, full of discovery ...
>
> Arriving there is what you are destined for.
> But do not hurry the journey at all.
> Better if it lasts for years ...
>
> Ithaka gave you the marvellous journey.
> Without her you would not have set out.
> She has nothing left to give you now.

Perhaps such a view also applies to our open-ended, interminable yet always terminated, psychoanalytic journeys.

*CHAPTER SIX*

# The year 2000

*The world's great age begins anew,*
*The golden years return ...*

Percy B. Shelley: *Hellas* 1822
1060–1061

The fantasy of witnessing the turn of the millennium was important to me, as I believed it was to many others of my genera-tion, belonging to cultures not only adopting the same Gregorian calendar[1] as we do, but also sharing with us a mostly linear experience of time. Such temporality, dominant throughout the urban-industrial world, is consistent with one of its central tenets, the illusory idea of progress, and is intrinsically different from the circular time prevalent in rural societies built around seasonal and biological rhythms.

\* \* \*

Those born in the first thirty years of the last century who have lived long enough to see the third millennium, have only done so in their old age and have mostly felt they belonged to the second one; while those born in the last ten or twenty years of the last century have to

65

a large extent experienced themselves as children already of the new millennium, because it was in it that they had reached maturity and spent most of their lives.

My generation, by which I mean those of us who were born in the middle part of the twentieth century, is in at least one respect unique: we could have realistically expected to witness in the course of our own "time odyssey" (to paraphrase the title of a well known film by Stanley Kubrick) the end of the old millennium and the beginning of the new one. We all have in common this temporal connection, if nothing else, like Salman Rushdie's (1981) "Midnight's children", who shared the destiny of being born on the night when their country achieved independence. This unusual feature might make some feel that they are rather exceptional. Fantasies of being special, though, are always charged with ambivalence: we both enjoy and feel guilty about them. In fact, we have an ambiguous attitude towards anything that makes us different from others. On the one hand we want to conform and be like everyone else, and on the other we try to differentiate ourselves from others and be identified by them for whatever our special features might be.

We can recognise in this ambivalent wish the omnipotent narcissistic fantasy of being chosen (by God, by fate, by one's parents) which magically makes the elect one a superior being, endowed with unique powers, or the recipient of special gifts. In our case, this fantasy can be interpreted as the manifestation of an unconscious need to belong to a watershed generation or community, like the chosen people led by Moses across the Red Sea, destined to be present in the year 2000 at the remarkable event of a universal birthday.

We know anniversaries to be meaningful. Their main psychological feature is that they repeat earlier events, and they are therefore invested with similar emotional connotations to those pertaining to the past. In psychopathology, anniversary reactions—such as the experience of acute depression on the occasion of the anniversary of a traumatic event, for instance the painful loss of an object or of its love—are well studied clinical phenomena. They are the unconscious response to such a reinvestment of emotional energy, "in the form of mastery through re-experience rather than through remembering" (Mintz, 1971). In other words, they are a specific instance of the phenomenon of repetition compulsion.

Of all anniversaries, birthdays and New Year's days, as we learn since childhood, deserve exceptional celebrations—rites of passage of a sort—which differentiate them from other days of the year. The first day of January of a new decade or, say, one's thirtieth or fiftieth birthday, are even more special, times maybe for reviews of past events, thorough and mostly useless, if not damaging, medical check-ups (see Illich, 1975), and long-term plans and resolves for the future. The unusual case of becoming a centenarian or the beginning of a new century are of course even more unique events.

If, in this hypothetical scale of importance, a decennial celebration is then more special than a yearly one, and that of a century is more important than that of a decade, it is not surprising that the beginning of a millennium should be considered a very extraordinary event indeed. This special quality is then magically transferred, without losing all the ambivalence pertaining to it, to those who happen to take part in such events: to the "birthday boy", to those who attended the celebrations for Queen Victoria's Golden Jubilee in the year 1887, to the 100-year-old lady being interviewed on the local television news and receiving a special royal birthday card, and to those like myself who have been privileged to see the new millennium in.

* * *

We all knew, of course, that the first day of the third millennium was unlikely to be any more different from the last day of the second millennium than today is from yesterday. And yet, in our unconscious minds dominated by magical thinking and primary process logic, this rational consideration simply does not apply. On the morning of her birthday, the little girl is convinced that she is one year older than she was the previous day, and she looks at herself in the mirror to find out how much taller she has grown ...

When we try to analyse this irrational belief, we find that it is related to the common fantasy of death and resurrection, of which the myth of Jesus Christ is probably the most powerful instance in our culture. This omnipotent fantasy, in turn, might originate from the unconscious wish to kill the old, the father, in order to give birth to the new, the son, and thus perpetuate the species.

These fantasies, repeating the basic pattern of separation and individuation (Mahler, Pine & Bergman, 1975) in toddlers and adolescents, are commonly expressed in mythology and literature, and can be observed in countless forms of human behaviour. Once we obtain a university degree, or lose our virginity (see Chapter Three), or get married (or divorced) everything will change. We shall clean the slate once we emigrate to a new country, or get out of prison. We shall start a new life once the war is over, or once we find our true love … "Magnus ab integro saeclorum nascitur ordo" ("The great succession of centuries is born afresh"), are Virgil's words from his messianic *Eclogue IV* (Virgil, c.40 BC), indicating this sense of universal hope.

But we have first to successfully overcome a time of crisis, that stage of transition between two different political, social, or psychological organisations, when the old one has not been totally abandoned and the new one has not yet been adopted. From my work back in the 1970s as a resident psychotherapist in a crisis intervention centre,[2] I have learnt that a crisis can become a turning point in a person's life, provided that enough time, space, and caring efforts are devoted to understanding its deeper meanings. In this sense, the experience and behaviour of someone undergoing a crisis—however incomprehensible, mad, or frightening they might at first appear to be—can be understood and treated as the expression of a need for radical changes, as a healthy manoeuvre for bringing about a psychological and social transformation, as a truly new beginning that follows a regression "to a point before the faulty development started" (Balint, 1968, p. 132).

Some amount of destruction of the old might of course be necessary in order to generate the new, but there is abundant historical evidence that revolutionary movements that mostly focus on the annihilation of the overthrown system instead of investing sufficient energies in creating a new one are doomed to failure. Yet, this is just what seems to happen in our fantasy life, possibly out of ancestral fears of parental envious revenge. Ultimately, the introjected "father" who has been the object of our ambivalent feelings and identifications has to be destroyed as a symbol of the past. This also serves the function of preventing him from destroying us in retaliation for our own original oedipal wishes and rage, in an unending chain of generational hostility, envy, jealousy, rebelliousness, and anger. But, out of this, the potential love towards the next generation is freed and made available. Thus, both the destructive and the creative instinctual tendencies, Thanatos and Eros, can be expressed. Every 500 years the phoenix is reborn from its own ashes.

\* \* \*

There seems to be something exciting about belonging to a generation that stretches across two millennia. What is it? We are left, perhaps, with the illusory impression of not belonging to either; of being in a constant transitional state that would almost provide absolution from the responsibility of sharing ideological meanings, of affecting the social and political institutions to which we belong, of partaking of our own history, or indeed of being alive at all, as individuals and as members of our community. We would then feel suspended, so to speak, in a state of relative immortality, which would fit in well with the hardest-to-die of all our unconscious beliefs.

Alternatively, living in both millennia—as a giant standing with each foot on a continent—is exciting because it gives us the sensation of belonging to different and contrasting worlds: the one of the children and the one of the grown-ups, the one of the past and the one of the future, the one of the living and the one of the dead. This, as I have suggested above, could make one feel endowed with special powers, feeding those narcissistic fantasies of omnipotence which are undoubtedly reactions against unconscious fears of destruction, annihilation, and death, kept under check through magical control. Such a need for control can take on obsessional features: it would be easy, in fact, to identify an element of repetition compulsion in all periodical rituals and ceremonies celebrating the passage of time. Those related to numbers (such as 100 or 1,000 and their multiples) lend themselves particularly well to be used for such defensive purposes.

Furthermore, what I think was exciting for many people was not just living through two millennia, but also seeing them both joined together in a sort of intercourse. The present generation, then, could express through the voyeuristic fantasies of the primal scene the conflictual wish to enter the new millennium, as a child stealthily creeping into the parental room. The almost obsessional interest of many of our contemporaries in such cultural phenomena as science fiction and futurology can be considered as evidence for this hypothesis. Again, one belongs for a moment to both worlds in order not to feel excluded from either. One can be the child of the twentieth century watching himself identified with the adults of the twenty-first, or the other way round too, as is well documented by the rich iconography of the white-bearded old man being replaced on the stroke of midnight on New Year's Eve by an innocent and peaceful newborn babe.

Inevitably, though, such fantasies leave us full of guilt, charged as they are with instinctual aggressiveness. In describing Schreber's paranoid fantasies, Freud states that "the end of the world is the projection of this internal catastrophe; his subjective world has come to an end

since his withdrawal of his love from it" (Freud, 1911c, p. 70). The sense
of guilt needs channels through which it can be assuaged; the fantasy
of expiation through apocalyptic catastrophe, with its own destructive and self-destructive components, had become available for this
purpose around the year 2000, as it had already a millennium earlier.
Through a cathartic process, the biological sequence from birth to death
is reversed, as it is indeed in all religious systems providing a belief in a
life after death, in this or in another world.

* * *

Millenarianism is a specific instance of the myth, common in many
cultures, of the Golden Age. The mechanisms operating here are the
denial of present aggressive and libidinal wishes experienced as greed
and therefore unacceptable, and the projection of them into a mythical,
a-historical time (past or future) when they were or will be fulfilled.
Interestingly, this Golden Age, or paradise lost, or future heaven, which
is so closely related to the fantasy of a blissful time preceding or following a certain crucial date (say the year 2000, or one's birth or death)
shares with our unconscious life the characteristic of being timeless—
a feature that also manifests itself in early childhood, when the infant
is still unable to negotiate the differentiation of the self—invested with
narcissistic omnipotence—from the external world, and has not yet
learned to relate to a multidimensional time.

Under normal circumstances, in our culture we tend to experience
time as a continuous and irreversible flow, from the past via the present
to the future. Not unlike death itself, the year 2000, which I have referred
to as watershed, is also a wall in this continuum, an unrequested stop.
The demarcation between the two millennia is sharp and colours our
experience of ourselves in time, as well as our relationship and commitment to history.

In the minds of the men and women of my generation and my culture, something quite tangible has come to an end before that fence;
and something else, an exciting and frightening unknown, has begun
beyond it. Some of our psychoanalytic patients have presented us with
their fantasies about the new millennium, much as they normally do
when they let their inner world and our consulting rooms be invaded
by such events as the trial of a child murderer, or the latest royal wedding. I remember that in 1984 I had a glimpse from behind the couch
of the popular significance of momentous dates simply because George

Orwell had chosen that year as the title for his novel (Orwell, 1949). The awareness of its entirely irrational importance went then well beyond the boundaries of political fiction.

About the unexplored world beyond the Pillars of Hercules, the Latins used to say "*Hic sunt leones*" (The lions are there). Or, maybe, there is something more terrifying than any wild beast could be. A nothingness, that is, which reflects our most primitive fears of an internal void and of irreversible annihilation.

A friend tells me the following dream:

> I am running away from something and I feel very scared that it might catch up with me. I finally reach a door, open it, and find myself in a corridor at the opposite end of which I can see another door. I would like to run to it and try to open it, but I think it might be locked. I am frightened of letting go of the first door, because if I did so it would shut before I could run back to it and I might then end up trapped in the corridor. Indeed, paralysed as I am in my indecision, still holding on to the first door handle, and hearing my enemy getting nearer, I am already hopelessly lost. At this point I wake up in a state of panic.

We become stuck in the present corridor when obstacles are erected between ourselves and a future which, rather than being a temporal dimension integrated in our actual experience, becomes a subject for pseudo-religious superstitions, science-fictional illusions, or speculations for futurologists. It is almost like having no future, no hope, an unreachable door ahead of us. We are, like my friend in her dream, petrified into statues.

We might of course have learnt to counterbalance this despair by idealistically projecting beyond that wall of the year 2000 all our aspirations and hopes. "People usually escape from their troubles into the future," writes the Czech novelist Milan Kundera, "They draw an imaginary line across the path of time, a line beyond which their current troubles will cease to exist" (Kundera, 1984, p. 165). One of the consequences of this psychological manoeuvre, though, is that we would have ended up feeling empty and deprived, as we tended to disinvest the last years of the twentieth century of any deeper historical significance, as reflected for instance in the deceptively reassuring cultural shambles of postmodernism during that *fin de siècle*; we were bitterly disappointed afterwards, when we realised that our wishes were left unfulfilled.

Either way, we have found ourselves in a no-man's-land, in a timeless kind of present (very different from the infantile omnipresent because, unlike children, we do know how to differentiate time into its dimensions) where the past has become meaningless and the future frightening, the one being disconnected from the other.

\* \* \*

In the case of the millenarian fantasy, the defensive function of mythologies, well researched by anthropologists and psychoanalysts, is exemplified by the illusion of controlling the unacceptable parts of ourselves in a magical and timeless past, where there was no suffering, separation, or frustration. Alternatively, we can nurse the illusion of getting rid of all our intolerable feelings by pushing them away into a mythical future time (old age, after-death, the year 1000 or 2000), only to become terrified again by their "return" as the time gets nearer and more real. Intrinsically, the two are only the opposite sides of the same coin, different aspects of the same psychological need to keep instinctual impulses under control.

Promises about a blissful future or threats about the disasters to come, and the belief in them, predominate in many religions. For instance, Pope John Paul II's encyclical letter on the Holy Ghost in 1986 was an appeal to the "threatened humanity" to react to "the picture of death which is being drawn in our times". The language is one of mystical apocalypse; the content is that of what Pope Wojtyla himself called "a new eschatology". The Pope's millenarian rhetoric is not unknown to many secular politicians either; in the years preceding the end of the second millennium their messages were centred with increased frequency around the myth of the year 2000, though each of them might have been preying upon different aspects of their audiences' primitive fantasies. Let me quote a few instances of this phenomenon. In his speech to the United Nations in 1981, the then Soviet foreign minister Andrej Gromiko proclaimed: "We must do all we possibly can for men to live in peace during the two remaining decades of the twentieth century, so that they could step across the threshold of the third millennium not loaded with worries about the future of civilisation, but full of hope in its unlimited potentials for development." Ronald Reagan, the then American President, told a pro-Israeli lobbyist in 1983: "I turn back to your ancient prophets in the Old Testament and the signs foretelling Armageddon, and I find myself wondering if we are the generation that's going to see that come about." And the then British Prime Minister

Margaret Thatcher, forecasting in her speech at the 1986 Conservative Party Conference that the Tories would stay in power until the year 2001, stated: "As we look forward to the next century, we have a vision of the society we wish to see," and she earned herself a nine-and-a-half-minute standing ovation.

Interestingly, historical records are replete with instances of movements of a millennial character where the failure of the prophecy (say, of the coming of the Messiah by a certain date) and the disconfirmation of the beliefs built around it bring about, against all logical expectations, an increased commitment to the ideology and a new fervour about convincing and converting others to it (see Festinger, Riecken & Schatter, 1956). The opportunity to move away from irrationality turns into an excuse for further plunging into it.

* * *

Of the many prophecies that can be interpreted as foretelling doomsday for the end of the second millennium, the most celebrated are those of Saint Malachi, who predicted in the twelfth century that John Paul would be the last but one Pope before the end of the world, and of the Yorkshire seer Mother Shipton who, four centuries later, announced that the world would end in 1991. But probably the most impressive prophecy of them all is the one made by the French physician and astrologist Michel de Nostredame (Nostradamus) who, in the middle of the sixteenth century, predicted that, "In the Year Nineteen Hundred and Ninety Nine and Seven Months from the Sky will Come a Great and Terrible King" (*Centuries*, X:72; quoted in McCann, 1984, p. 346). In Christianity, the well-known passage of "The Apocalypse" from St. John's *The Revelation* (Chapter XX) predicts 1,000 years of peace followed by the flooding of the forces of Satan:

> And I saw an angel come down from heaven, having the key of the bottomless pit and a great chain in his hand. And he laid hold on the dragon, that old serpent, which is the Devil, and Satan, and bound him a thousand years, and cast him into the bottomless pit, and shut him up, and set a seal upon him, that he should deceive the nations no more, till the thousand years should be fulfilled: and after that he must be loosed a little season ...

The French leading medievalist Georges Duby expressed in his brilliant essay "*L'An Mil*", from which I shall here quote several times, the commonly held opinion that this chapter of *The Revelation* provided "a key to a chronology of the future" (Duby, 1967, p. 26), that it was "the foundation of millenarianism" (Duby, 1967, p. 27). I would suggest that the dread about the end of the world in the year 1000 did not derive from a reading of John's *Apocalypse*, but from a deeper unconscious terror about individual and collective separation and death. In the case of the beginning of the second millennium, such fears then found *a posteriori* justification in the passages from the Holy Scripture.

Our historical knowledge of the years around the beginning of the eleventh century is limited. The only documents available to us concerning those years are some *Annals*, where the main known events were registered year by year (and those about the year 1000 itself are most scanty); some *Chronicles*, such as the famous ones by Adhémar de Chabannes, which were literary versions of the Annals; two *Books of Miracles*, compound writings about the wonders worked by the virtue of the Holy Bodies; and finally, three *Histories*, the most famous of which is that of Radulfus Glaber, by far the best witness of his times. It is interesting to note that, although modern historians, such as Bloch (1939) and Focillon (1952), have seriously questioned what Duby calls "the Romantic opinion" that around the year 1000 people were terrified by the certain imminence of the end of the world, such an opinion still prevails today. Evidently, writes Duby, "in the collective conscience, the millenarian models have not altogether lost to-date their seductive qualities" (Duby, 1967, p. 5).

In fact, Duby falls into the same ambiguity he has identified in others. "When we examine the writings of contemporary historians, we are surprised to find that most of them attribute but little importance to the one-thousandth year from the Incarnation. It passed unnoticed." But then he adds: "Undoubtedly, though, on the threshold of the eleventh century, a feeling of expectation nestled inside the collective conscience" (Duby, 1967, p. 25). While dismissing the historical evidence for the "Romantic opinion" about the year 1000, Duby, using a series of fascinating excerpts from original sources, demonstrates the importance of the millenarian fantasy in our ancestors' minds.

In fact the whole tradition of revolutionary millenarianism and mystical anarchism, scholarly researched by Norman Cohn (1970) in his socio-historical study, developed in Western Europe in the course of the centuries *following* the year 1000. Brethren of the Free Spirit, Taborites, Anabaptists, Ranters have all been part of a complex ideological movement "in pursuit of the millennium". Between the eleventh and sixteenth centuries, writes Cohn, "the usual desire of the poor to improve the material conditions of their lives became transfused with phantasies of a world reborn into innocence through a final, apocalyptic massacre" (Cohn, 1970, p. 14). He suggests that the "millenarian movements of the medieval poor ... were true precursors of some of the great revolutionary movements of the present century" (Cohn, 1970, p. 15).

Duby describes the years preceding the beginning of the second millennium as being characterised in the Western world by "a highly hierarchical society, masses of slaves, a population of pitifully wretched farm-workers, entirely subjected to the rule of a few families" (Duby, 1967, p. 17). Day-to-day reality though, was of little interest to the historians, chroniclers, and annalists responsible for recording the events of those times. They seem to notice only what is exceptional, unusual, or odd, what breaks the orderly course of things and is therefore of specific divine or diabolical nature.

As the millenary of Christ's incarnation (1000) and that of his redemption (1033) get closer, great marvels are expected: "The tales of ancient historians", writes Duby, "had accustomed us to find it natural that the death of heroes—that is of the saints, the emperor and the kings—is accompanied by a suite of unusual phenomena. It seems therefore absolutely normal that, in memory of Christ, the millenary should be a time of the greatest of marvels" (Duby, 1967, p. 85).

The comet of the year 1014 and the solar eclipse of 29 June 1033 (millenary of the Passion) gave cosmic proportions to the ensuing chaos. This chaos was also biological, with the sighting of monsters, such as a whale of exceptional size, and the spreading of epidemics and famines, like the dramatic one in Burgundy in 1033 described by Radulfus Glaber. And finally this chaos was spiritual, with instances of simony and heretical ferments (the Manichaeans in Aquitania) and with the profanation in 1009 of the Church of the Holy Sepulchre in Jerusalem.

\* \* \*

What sort of cosmic, biological, and spiritual chaos, if any, did we expect to occur around the year 2000? This time gloomy predictions about the future of the human species, and indeed of life on our planet, were not based, as they were a millennium earlier, on superstitions or one-sided interpretations of a passage from the Scriptures, but on verifiable realities. My generation's widespread pessimism then was not related to the approaching of the year 2000, but was rationally justifiable by the current technological misuse of scientific knowledge (irreversible, unlike most political decisions), which was and is still making our self-destruction possible, and perhaps unavoidable, in a near future. Psychoanalysts, prominent among them Hanna Segal (1987), contributed in those years to clarify the unconscious, as well as realistic, sources of those anxieties. In a study specifically focused on the expectations about the year 2000 among young and older subjects, Reale found that adolescents "stress technological progress and ecological problems, as well as wars and political changes ... Adults have a much more pessimistic view about it: they talk about catastrophes, chaos, something entirely negative" (Reale, 1984, p. 199).

What I want to emphasise here is a confusion that I think has occurred between millenarian apocalyptic fears—which, as we have seen, belong to the realm of irrationality, narcissistic fantasies, unconscious guilt and need for expiation—on the one hand and, on the other, the reality of the destruction that we, civilised human beings, have with remarkable short-sightedness been bringing upon ourselves and our environment through massive ecological violence and the race, only recently slowed down, towards a nuclear holocaust.

This confusion ("from the Sky will Come a Great and Terrible King") involves a perilous concealment of the very facts and their potential consequences which we must instead be clearly aware of if we have any chance of preventing what many already believe to have become inevitable. Too easily do we become blind, or indifferent, to the systematic destruction of our natural habitat, too readily do we accept that there is no way out of the dangerous paradox of nuclear deterrence, too deep and widespread is among us a self-defeating attitude towards our future, combining helplessness and diffidence, naivety and bitterness.

In the last ten to twenty years before the third millennium we witnessed the growth of irrational religious and ideological movements centred around the new millenarian superstition, which has contributed to even more confusion and ignorance about the issues crucial to our survival,[3] thus further paralysing many into hopelessness and acquiescence.

I can only indicate here a few tips of the frighteningly enormous sub-cultural iceberg of such ideologies. Millions of fundamentalists throughout the United States shared a fascination for the belief that Armageddon was imminent, which Mojtabai (1986) called "end-time thinking" and attributed both to the nuclear arms race and to the coming of the year 2000. Widespread right-wing groups of so-called survivalists, both in America and in Britain, spend their time in paramilitary self-defence training, preparing for the end of the world. An organisation called Worldwide Church distributes every month over seven million copies (300,000 in Britain alone) of its magazine *Plain Truth*. Frank Brown, one of this church's directors, explained its central belief: "We are getting towards the end of man's time. The Bible tells us of certain signs that prophesy this. We want to spread understanding of those signs and why they are appearing" (from *The Guardian* 9 March 1987). Huge armies of Jehovah's Witnesses believe that "world events in fulfilment of prophecy show that we are deep into the 'last days' ... However, the approach of Armageddon should not be a cause for fear, but for real hope! Why? Because Armageddon is God's war to cleanse the earth of all wickedness, paving the way for a prosperous new order!" (quoted in Humphrey and Lifton, 1984, p. 85).

On their part the mass-media had contributed to fuelling collective hysteria—or is it paranoia?—by daily feeding their readers tabloid newspaper headlines such as "AIDS, plague of the year 2000". A few months before the end of the century I received a circular letter promoting a new savings plan: "Cash Booster 2001. Get ready to welcome the 21st Century now! And receive a superb leather wallet free! ... When you reach the 21st Century you'll be glad you invested in Cash Booster 2001!"

Our ancestors of a thousand years ago were at least spared this. The responsibility of the men of the Church, Pope Sylvester II with his abbots and monks, was to interpret signs and marvels, to understand their meanings and reveal them to the people. These men, who hated and despised the Manichaeans, were themselves imbued with an instinctual dualism, as they were "tempted to consider the general perturbation, which then manifests itself in so many different forms and shapes, as a victory for the Devil" (Duby, 1967, p. 109). We now know, and Duby also stresses this point, that "one-thousand years gone by, and all disasters being over, Christianity emerged, so to speak, from a new baptism. Order followed chaos. The day after the year one-thousand is a new spring for the whole world" (Duby, 1967, p. 151), opening the gates to the blooming of Renaissance.

Despite an unpromising start with prolonged wars (Iraq, Afghanistan, Syria), major acts of terrorism (9/11) and extensive economic crisis in its first decade, we could only hope for the new millennium that "the other of the two 'Heavenly Powers', eternal Eros, will make an effort to assert himself in the struggle with his equally immortal adversary" (Freud, 1930a, p. 145). Ultimately, it is up to us.

*CHAPTER SEVEN*

# On the couch

*I cannot put up with being stared at*
*by other people for eight hours a day.*

—Sigmund Freud: On beginning the treatment 1913
*Standard Edition*, Vol. 12, p. 134

Having so far dwelled on various aspects of the temporal dimension of psychoanalysis, I shall now focus on the analytic space as the physical and psychological *locus* where the analytic process occurs. Our obvious starting point must be the analytic consulting room itself, with its specific features, a space characterised by its "freedom of speech" made possible by its safe boundaries.

\* \* \*

One person sits in a chair, mostly listening. The other one lies on a couch, mostly talking.

This is the apparently simple situation we are familiar with, having been ourselves sitting in such chairs and lying on such couches for years. There seems to be something special about this artificial setting which facilitates the establishment and development of that unique human relationship that is the psychoanalytic one. As one of my analysands once put it, "The beauty of the couch is in the fact that it *unhinges* the normal, face-to-face way of having a conversation. It allows what happens here to be something different, something quite special."

Here I shall focus on the couch; for lying on it, or resisting doing so, has profound meanings and wide-ranging implications for both participants in the analytic process.

Historically, that "certain ceremonial" of asking patients to lie on a couch is "the remnant of the hypnotic method out of which psychoanalysis was evolved" (Freud, 1913c, p. 133). The analyst sits in a chair behind the couch, in a position out of sight from the patient.[1]

Asking the analysand to lie on the couch can be seen as "a modification of the attempt to put the patient to sleep" (Greenson, 1967, p. 409) which was a precondition for hypnotherapy. Of course we do not intend to put our psychoanalytic patients to sleep—quite the contrary!—though they do sometimes sleep.[2] What is true is that by inducing a state of relaxation through the recumbent position we encourage a certain amount of regression, which facilitates the free-associative process, a more immediate contact with unconscious material, and the emergence of transference dynamics.

It seems that the reclining position of the patient, combined with the analyst sitting out of his sight, is such a powerful therapeutic tool mostly because it confronts the analysand with a creative ambiguity: Is the patient talking to his analyst or to himself?

Let me report as illustration the following fragment from Albert's analysis:

> Albert starts the session by referring to what the previous day he had called his "emotional stinginess", that is his difficulty in expressing gratitude. I say that he seems to be warning me that, like his parents, I should not expect any gratitude from him. Albert replies that he does not see me as a person, but just as an analyst and *therefore* he does not feel that I deserve any particular praise, nor—he adds reassuringly—any criticism. After all, Albert goes on to say, he is not really talking to me but to himself. After a short pause, I suggest a link between this statement and the fact that today is the last session before the Easter break. Yes, he says, he doesn't think he could just lie down for fifty minutes every day for the next two weeks and talk to himself without me. But why not? What is the difference?

That baffles him! Maybe, Albert's monologue continues, it is the routine, the imposition of a formal setting, like having to attend a class to study a foreign language: you don't learn much at the lessons themselves, but you know that without them you just would not study the language and learn it.

(Albert reminded me here of another patient who, having seen a "For sale" sign on the fence near my front gate, at first panicked at the thought that I was moving out, then realised that the sign related to the terraced house next to mine. At this point she expressed the fantasy that she would buy the next-door house herself, furnish its top-floor room exactly like mine, lie on the couch there for fifty minutes at the same times and on same days as she comes to see me, and save herself quite a lot of money.)

Patients are faced with the outer world of their projections and, at the same time, with the inner one of introjections; with the relationship both to a real person and, through the transference, to their own internal objects. The couch forces them, or rather helps them though they often resist it, to become the listeners to their own words, the observers of their own minds, in ways that would not be possible in the face-to-face position. At the same time the invisible presence and disembodied voice of the analyst behind them, a situation not unlike that of a parent being next-door to the toddler's playroom, provides an element of security and a link with the here-and-now of reality which complements the regression, the primary process "madness", the timeless atmosphere and the narcissistic isolation of the session, and also contains them.

The literature on the couch is scanty, though most books and papers on psychoanalytic technique make some reference to it. The main articles I found dealing directly with this issue are those of Kelman (1954) who describes the couch in terms of the analytic setting and explores whether the couch is better than the chair; Hall and Closson (1964) who report that experienced judges, when listening to tape-recorded sessions, could not differentiate those in which the patients were sitting up from those in which they were lying down, even though the judges themselves were confident that they could; Robertiello (1967) who sees the couch as a tool by which the therapist defends himself from emotional involvement with his patients; and Gruen (1967) who, in response to Robertiello, cautions against confusing the couch with the person: a good therapist should be capable of interacting with his patients regardless of whether they sit on a chair or lie on a couch. Rosenbaum (1967) explores the symbolic meaning, the benefits, and the limitations of the couch. A monographic issue of *Psychoanalytic Inquiry* about the couch included papers by Frank (1995), Aruffo (1995) and Grotstein (1995). Other articles on this topic are by Celenza (2005), Schachter and Kächele (2010), Lingiardi and Bei (2011), and a recent research project started by Lable et al. (2010).

Stern is the author of the only comprehensive textbook I know of which is focused entirely on this subject. His attitude about the use of the couch is flexible; he explores in great detail its historical origins and cultural significance—"an ever-present reminder and indeed a symbol of (the analyst's) work" (Stern, 1978, p. 13)—and he emphasises the importance of its meaning for both analyst and analysand in the context of their therapeutic relationship.

Whether patients verbally express it or not, they usually have strong feelings at the suggestion to use the couch. Some comply straightaway without a word of protest. Others, like Bruna, the patient I shall describe here below in some detail, refuse to lie on it for a period of time, adducing a variety of reasons to justify their resistance to following the analyst's suggestion. Both behaviours (the "compliant" and the "rebellious") require careful analysis, as they are likely to be transferential repetitions of earlier attitudes towards authority figures. Some believe that the analysts' own reasons for asking patients to lie on the couch should also be scrutinised, as there could be in them "seductive and hostile motives, and needs to make the patient unduly subservient" (Langs, 1973, p. 177); or they could use it defensively to protect themselves from erotic or aggressive countertransference feelings that would thus fail to be analysed.

As to the appropriateness of using the couch at all, as opposed to sitting face-to-face in a chair, two distinctions are often made. The first one is between neurotic patients who can and should lie on the couch, and borderline or psychotic ones who cannot and should not, on the grounds that the reclined position would encourage forms of malignant regression with the emergence of intolerable anxiety and the loss of reality-testing.

> Celia, a borderline patient of mine whom I have been seeing in analysis for several years, told me that when she was an adolescent she had a consultation with a psychoanalyst who had asked her to

lie on the couch. As she replied that she did not want to, he told her that she was "un-analysable" and that she should therefore "seek a different sort of treatment". I assume that the rationale of this rigid analyst was that anyone resisting lying on the couch must be too disturbed to be helped by psychoanalysis.[3]

The second distinction offered by some clinicians is the one between psychoanalysis which should take place on the couch, and psychotherapy which should not. This point seems to me logically weak, in so far as the use of the couch is itself one of the main elements defining psychoanalysis as distinct from psychotherapy. Were we to be asked, "Is this young woman in psychoanalysis because she is on the couch, or is she on the couch because she is in psychoanalysis?", which answer could we then give? Whatever the validity of such distinctions, I believe that there should be flexibility over this issue. The analyst should recommend it without insisting on either position, as her main concern should not be about *where* her patients put their bodies, but *why*. What matters about the couch is its meaning within the analytic relationship, which varies from patient to patient and at different stages of the analysis.

A psychotherapy patient of mine, a very inflexible person rigidly sitting on the chair in front of me, expressed in the course of a session the hope that one day he would trust me enough to be able to lie on the couch. It was a remarkable coincidence that only a few hours later another patient of mine, a very dependent older man with a history of passive homosexuality, expressed from the couch the wish that one day he would feel strong enough to sit up, move to the chair opposite mine and bravely face me "man-to-man". For both these patients, therapeutic success consisted of moving from a position that they considered to be symptomatic of their pathology to one that, for them, represented the overcoming of their problems. As Stern points out, the object "is not principally to get the patient on the couch, but to resolve the emotional conflicts that are represented in the resistances" (Stern, 1978, p. 156).

To illustrate the overdetermined significance of this aspect of the analytic setting, which might on the surface appear to be a merely technical one, I shall now use some clinical material from Bruna, a woman in her mid-thirties who sat on my couch for the first sixteen months of her analysis, unable to lie on it until enough therapeutic work was done about the numerous aspects of her resistance. Bruna could have chosen to sit in the more comfortable chair face-to-face to me, but she opted for the awkward sitting position on the couch as a compromise that, from the beginning, indicated to me the presence of a complex conflictual situation. It was as if, in response to my suggestion in the course of the preliminary interview that she would have probably found it helpful to lie on the couch, Bruna had answered: "Yes, I would like to, but I cannot!", or, maybe: "Of course I could, but I don't want to!"

I did not insist then, guessing that, if I had, she would have been likely to comply, but that we would have missed an opportunity to explore and understand important aspects of her personality and psychopathology. As her analysis progressed, the issue of the couch kept cropping up many times, its links with various aspects of the transference becoming increasingly clear. In the countertransference I found myself feeling at times anxious for a resolution of her ambivalence, at times irritated by her incapacity to follow such a simple request, and at times guilty for being unable to enforce it with her.

I shall now delineate some of the main areas of conflict pertaining to Bruna's resistance to the lying posture as I believe that they are in a sense universal for all analytic patients, although the intensity of the emotions involved and the form of their manifestation are specific to the woman I am describing. It could be argued that the clinical material I shall here present is an illustration not so much of the experience of lying on the couch (such as feeling relaxed, vulnerable, lost, lonely, peaceful, frightened, omnipotent), but rather of some of the resistances to it. Yet it seems to me that even those patients who consciously comply with that tenet of the analytic setting which is lying on the couch are often in a state of conflict over it, though this is more unlikely to come immediately and concretely into their material, and therefore it often fails to be analysed. In this sense we can learn something important *on* the couch from those analysands who are *off* it.

Bruna told me in the course of one of her first sessions that lying on the couch would have been for her like having sexual intercourse. She proceeded to describe it as something awful, in which she would have been "passive and uninvolved". In response to my comment that she seemed to be talking about an abusive encounter, she reported a memory from her early adolescence: a "friend" had pushed her against a wall and had asked her to touch his penis. She was clearly worried that I would similarly corner her by taking advantage of the couch, were she to lie on it, in order to somehow abuse her.[4] As it later emerged, Bruna feared being unexpectedly and gratuitously attacked, which was related to her early experiences of being physically punished by her parents, often without being warned beforehand or given any explanations afterward. In this sense, having me behind her was tantamount to giving me the power to repeat the traumatic situations she had suffered in her childhood.

When, later in her analysis, Bruna developed a markedly erotic transference towards me, the fear of being raped was replaced by a wish to be seduced. In this fantasy the predominant features were of a pregenital nature, with emphasis on hugging, holding hands, physical closeness and tenderness, which I interpreted as her wish to have with me in the present the intimate relationship that, as a child, she had longed for in vain from her distant parents. Again, these fantasies involved lying with me on the couch and were associated to the memory of her mother lying next to her in bed to help her go to sleep.

Around the same period Bruna expressed the thought that her head, were she to lie down, would have been too near to me, again suggesting that she still felt threatened by physical proximity, probably because of its oedipal connotations, as the initial sadomasochistic component of the rape fantasy had by then lost its intensity. It is interesting to note that Bruna invariably sat on the couch keeping her legs crossed and her hands locked together over her knees—almost to further protect herself from the imagined attempts on my part to penetrate her sexually, as well as a concrete symbolic expression of her defensiveness against my penetrating interpretations.

Another important aspect of Bruna's resistance to lying on the couch was her fear of finding herself out of control, helpless like a child, engulfed, overwhelmed by intense feelings from which she could not have protected herself and me. Her resistance meant also that she felt physically trapped, that she could not have run away from my consulting room as quickly as she could have from the sitting position. Since the death of a close friend from a pulmonary disease Bruna had always been sensitive to anything that she experienced as suffocating or limiting her freedom of movements. She once felt that she was going to faint on the couch and talked about a friend who had recently suffered a heart attack. Indeed, lying down on the couch represented for her falling asleep, dreaming, giving into regressive fantasies and emotions, and even dying.

Linked to both themes of sexuality and loss of control was Bruna's anxiety of not seeing me from the reclining position. The couch in analysis facilitates the withdrawal of visual attention from the outside by hindering the sight of the analyst. The visual component, which plays such an important part in normal relationships, is to a large extent replaced in psychoanalysis by an intensification of the verbal and auditory ones. Often the tone of the analyst's voice becomes then a factor of great significance for the patient, who thus runs the risk of taking as communicative something which is just expressive. For Bruna the exploratory curiosity of the child who wants to learn how things work or where they come from, and the scopophilic fantasies around the primal scene were inseparable. Before one of her first sessions, she managed to open several doors in my house looking for the toilet, though I had explained to her where it was. We are not surprised to find such voyeuristic tendency to be accompanied by its opposite, exhibitionistic ones. Let me report a vignette from a session with Bruna, after nearly one year of analysis.

> "I have been thinking about lying down", she said, "but I don't think I could stand actually doing it. It's so embarrassing! I would feel watched by you ... I couldn't stand it, unless maybe you turned your back to me so that you wouldn't see me! I don't know what others do, if they wrap themselves up in the blanket when they feel cold, if they take their shoes off ..." I say that she seems to feel as if she had to undress in front of me, to expose something very intimate that she feels embarrassed about. "Oh yes", she agrees, "the couch has always had to do with sexuality for me. I am afraid of what your wishes about me could be ... or, actually, my wishes about you".

Bruna needed to see me, though only edgewise from her sitting position on the couch, in order to make sure that I would not abandon her, as well as to monitor my facial expression and my reactions to her words, hoping that she could thus find signs that I liked her, that I shared her joys and sorrows, that I worried about her problems as her parents never had. This continued to play an important part later, as Bruna used the moments before and after each session to observe me carefully and take clues from my way of greeting her in the waiting room or of saying "goodbye" to her upon her leaving. Two days after starting to lie down, Bruna told me that she had hoped that I would move from my chair to the one opposite it where she could have kept in visual contact with me.

It was not just the wish to see me that for many months prevented Bruna from lying on the couch; it was also the fact that she could not see me *while I could see her* (in fact, from my angle, I could only see her hair, one shoulder, and her shoes sticking up!). This evoked deep resentment in her about what she called the one-sidedness of our relationship; envy about feeling inferior to me, experiencing herself as passive and powerless as a patient in relation to an analyst, as a woman in relation to a man, as a "little girl" in relation to her father; feeling excluded, as she so often had as a child, from all the exciting things which, once more, were happening behind her back. Rebelling then against this one analytic rule became for Bruna a condensed version of her struggle against passivity, compliance and obedience, and against her impotence for being, in the transference, the child who could not get what she wanted from her parents.

In the course of the first sixteen months Bruna often admitted that she would have liked lying on my couch. She once remembered envying her cousins (my other patients) who had a garden and could just lie down on deckchairs (my couch), relax and have a good time in the sunshine (in analysis). It would have been pleasant, soothing, and resting for her too; but she could not let herself do it, in so far as she experienced it as a personal favour to me. "No, I couldn't lie on this couch!", she emphatically stated after fourteen months of analysis. "I must oppose you at some level in order to keep control, not to give into your expectations and feel exploited. If I lay down I would feel totally taken for granted; you would claim a victory over me and feel triumphant. Then I would become a patient!" Interestingly, she often talked about the loss of her virginity and about her giving into men's sexual wishes in exactly the same terms.

The shift from the sitting to the lying position happened unexpectedly. I was aware that much analytic work had been done about it in the previous months and that some of the obstacles had been removed. Nevertheless, I found myself surprised the day when, sitting on my chair, I realised that for the first time after 279 sessions Bruna was not sitting parallel to me in the middle of the couch, her legs crossed and hands locked over them, but was rigidly lying on it, in a silence full of expectation and tension. Then she simply announced: "I have decided to lie down." After a pause I asked her what had made her reach this decision, for I thought it was as important now for us to understand why she lay on the couch as it had been previously to understand why she could not do so. This question of mine, as I later realised, was probably premature and motivated in part by my own feelings of shock about the new situation, but it was also intended as an acknowledgement to Bruna of her making such a step. She tried to defensively minimise this development in her analysis by answering that, having felt so helpless recently, she was convinced that nothing would ever change and that I could not really be of much help to her; she, then, had to do something radical herself. Yet, even then, she wished that I would have explicitly asked her to lie on the couch, as this would have reinforced her self-image of being the victim of external circumstances and given her further reasons for self-righteous resentment against me. Interestingly enough for someone I had always considered to have a passive-aggressive personality, Bruna once explained her reluctance to use my couch by saying that from a lying position she could not have been *actively defensive*!

Since then, Bruna has always lain down during sessions, occasionally expressing the wish to turn her head around to see me and reassure herself that I had not vanished from my chair as so many others had from her life. Unlike my other patients, Bruna used to rush towards the couch and throw herself on it, in a stiff corpse-like position, before I could reach my chair. As if, she once told me, she might still have changed her mind about it, had she left herself enough time to consider it. In other words, at least some of her conflicts surrounding her use of the couch, that is, aspects of her relationship with me that had made it so difficult for her to take the recumbent position for many months, were still unresolved and required further psychoanalytic investigation.

* * *

The couch, which for the general public has come to represent the psychoanalytic profession itself, contributes to the therapeutic process by inducing a state of physical and psychological relaxation in the analysand and, indirectly, in the analyst too. On the couch, patients can feel encouraged to talk more freely about themselves, focusing on their internal world while external distractions are reduced, and analysts can better listen to them. Furthermore, lying on the couch facilitates the development of that creative ambiguity in the analytic discourse that I have referred to above. I do not believe, though, that the couch is in itself a panacea and that lying on it will bring therapeutic success whereas sitting on a chair would mean failure. What ultimately matters is the rapport that analyst and analysand can establish with each other, regardless of their relative position in the room. Within the analytic relationship the emphasis should shift from a dogmatic imposition of procedures, rules, and technical devices, such as the use of the couch, to the understanding of the specific meanings they assume within the transference for any given patient.

* * *

Before leaving the couch as the site *par excellence* of the psychoanalytic encounter, I would like to make at least a brief reference to that very different space which, in the course of these last few years, is becoming accepted, if not necessarily as a first choice, among many analysts, and which does away altogether with the problem of the couch.

For several years now many colleagues had been conducting telephone sessions with analysands and supervisees who lived too far away from their consulting rooms to attend in person, or who were incapacitated to do so for other justified reasons (Zalusky, 2003). Today, however, thanks to the introduction of, and easy access to, new electronic technologies things have progressed much further, with a rapidly growing number of analyses around the world taking place in a *virtual space*. The shared space in which analyst and patient can now meet is no longer a physical room, but a no less real one that only exists, however, in an electronically constructed, intangible world. The existence of such communication tools as Skype, which allow real-time and free visual as well as auditory contact, happens to combine the popularity of these means of communication, especially among the younger generations of "digital natives" (Prensky, 2001), with the progressing decrease in popularity of traditional psychoanalysis as a therapeutic form of intervention. This series of circumstances has meant that many analysts today are embracing, not of course without all sorts of caveats and doubts, the practice of conducting sessions in this virtual, couchless space.

International conferences, online debates and a vast literature on the subject of so-called "tele-analysis" are being produced (*e.g.*, Carlino, 2011; Lemma & Caparrotta, 2013), with all sorts of valid arguments being voiced both in favour of and against it. Only time will tell though, whether the demands made on our "analytic attitude" by such a radical transformation of the conventional setting is ultimately justified by the results obtained, and whether the couch on which we have learnt our impossible profession will ever be replaced by a computer screen.

*CHAPTER EIGHT*

# Possession anxiety

*I should myself expect that it is precisely the castration complex*
*that would be bound to arouse the most general repudiation.*
*But I can only insist that psycho-analytic experience*
*has put these matters in particular beyond the reach of doubt*
*and has taught us to recognize in them the key to every neurosis.*

—Sigmund Freud: Dostoevsky and parricide, 1928
*Standard Edition*, 21, p. 184

This chapter is intended as a step towards redressing an imbalance in that aspect of analytic thinking which too often seems to emphasise absence rather than presence. For instance, pleasure is often defined by psychoanalysts as being merely the absence of unpleasure; normality or mental health as absence of psychopathology; the woman's relationship to her body as characterised by desire or envy for something missing; and anxiety, especially in Freud's later formulation (1926d), as being mostly related to fear of losing the object or its love, rather than to possessing it.

91

Castration anxiety concerns the fantasy of the loss of something precious: "Male children suffer from a fear of being robbed of their sexual organ by their father, so that this fear of being castrated has a most powerful influence on the development of their character" (Freud, 1926e, p. 211). The vicissitudes of this anxiety are different in girls, "for though they have a castration complex they cannot have a fear of being castrated. Its place is taken in their sex by a fear of loss of love" (Freud, 1933a, p. 87). But even if the girl has never possessed a penis, she often imagines that she will have one when she grows older, or that she originally had one and now has to mourn its loss.

For all children, then, though perhaps more clearly for boys, the castration complex, of which castration anxiety is the most obvious manifestation, plays a central part in the oedipal constellation, as the feared or fantasised loss is experienced as punishment from the parent of the same sex for the forbidden oedipal wishes towards the other parent. "If the satisfaction of love in the field of the Oedipus complex is to cost the child his penis, a conflict is bound to arise between his narcissistic interest in that part of his body and the libidinal cathexis of his parental objects. In this conflict the first of these forces normally triumphs: the child's ego turns away from the Oedipus complex" (Freud, 1924d, p. 176).

However, it seems to me that human beings can experience anxiety not only about losing what they consider precious, but also about possessing what they consider dangerous. In other words, they feel not only the fear of an absence, but also the threat of a presence. I suggest calling this other side (or inverse) of the castration anxiety *possession anxiety*. Possession anxiety relates to the presence of an ambivalently charged object taking its power from the person possessing it, who will then fear losing control over the object. I shall here mention only in passing the fear of having a tumour, as different from the fear of dying of it, as a common instance of such an anxiety.

We should start by asking ourselves: are the male and female genitals, and all they symbolically stand for, necessarily experienced as precious objects that one is anxious about losing, or envious about others possessing? Or is it not rather the case that for some, if not for all, they could also be frightening objects (external and internal), the presence of which, in oneself and in others, can cause states of anxiety? The role they play, for instance, in relation to the ambivalence about the issue of virginity and its eventual loss, as we have seen in Chapter Three, is a case in point. After all, there must be an interrelationship between what is frightening and what is exciting: phobias are an obvious example of attempts at avoiding what is most dreaded precisely because it represents what is unconsciously most exciting. Such fusion of emotional connotations is only partially overcome during childhood in the context of a normal establishment and resolution of the Oedipus complex. In the experience of the child, the two parental objects of ambivalent investments tend to separate and then appropriate the one more distinctly exciting and the other more clearly threatening features.

For both boys and girls the phallus is a symbol of concrete power: power to control and master, power to satisfy needs and to destroy enemies, power to fulfil sadistic fantasies and narcissistic wishes of omnipotence. But phallic symbols of power are inevitably experienced as appropriating that power for themselves, and removing it from the persons who have them.

From an emotional point of view the genitals as part-objects seem then to assume almost a life of their own. Once they have become invested with power, a shift in one's sense of identity occurs whereby one starts to perceive and experience oneself and others with increased ambivalence and anxiety. For instance, a baby will realise that there is a mother behind the breast and will have to relinquish some of his primitive oral omnipotence. Gradually, the pregenital infant will become the oedipal child, and the parents, who were at first mainly experienced as asexual beings, now become a woman and a man. Later still the adolescent will feel overwhelmed by the anatomical and physiological changes of puberty and will undergo a critical developmental stage in the areas of separation–individuation and of the establishment of self-identity. And so on, throughout the life cycle.

Anxiety about possessing the genitals, as a more specific aspect of possessing a body, is related to the fear of the unknown. This in turn is unconsciously associated with sexual fantasies, with awe about something that has a life and a power of its own, that evokes exciting sensations and can generate children, and that has therefore deeply mysterious and at times frightening connotations. I would add here that the concept of possession anxiety might also help us to understand the development of the sense of shame, leading in most cultures to the covering up of the genitals: not only because we fear other people's envy of them and their wish to take them away from us (which of course includes a projective element), but also because, by not showing our sexual attributes, we can magically make them disappear, deny their existence and threatening qualities, and thus protect ourselves from the anxiety, of which shame would then be a particular instance.

Possession anxiety is, I believe, a normal phenomenon, but it is most obviously apparent in psychopathology, for example, in two forms of sexual perversion (transexualism and fetishism) and in anorexia nervosa.[1] The transexual person feels split between mind and body (or parts of it: the genitals), the latter being experienced as an inadequate physical representative or container of the former. The only solution available to transsexual people is a surgical operation, or the fantasy of some analogous magical procedure, to remove the evidence of a "wrong" body inside which they feel trapped, and endow it with new, more fitting and powerful sexual organs. This is the opposite of the experience of feeling possessed (by evil spirits, the devil, the soul of a dead person) where what has to be removed is not the body but its contents, through the magical operation of exorcism. Again, anxiety in these pathological conditions seems to be related more to the presence of something experienced as inadequate, frightening, inconsistent, or threatening than to the fear of losing it.

In fetishism, once more, it is the hated and feared genitals, both male and female, that are replaced by a more innocuous fetish, which often maintains only a tenuous symbolic association with the original object, but is more easily controlled and manipulated. The fetish "remains a token of triumph over the threat of castration and a protection against it" (Freud, 1927e, p. 154).

In anorexia nervosa we find another instance of a similar phenomenon. Here the whole body is experienced as the equivalent of the genitals (the whole for the part, so to speak) and as the evidence of the anorexic's sexual identity. Thus he, or more often she, has to deny it by hiding it away; starving it; torturing it; making it smaller, thinner, invisible; annihilating it—ultimately by killing it. The anorexic's "solution" to her problem does not stem from her anxiety of losing her body, but quite the opposite, from her anxiety of possessing it. Hence her wish, as the Italian proverb goes, *di vivere d'aria e d'amore*—"to live out of thin air and love". The specific existential dilemma of anorexics is related to the wider problem of identity, of which gender identity is but one aspect, and is intrinsically connected with the issue of power relations that I have referred to above. The problem here is a fear not only of *losing* one's identity and having to resort to defence mechanisms or to signal anxiety in order to protect it from external or internal threats, but also of *possessing* an identity, in so far as it commits one to a complex system of biological, psychological, sexual, and social functions and roles that one may fear being unable to adequately perform.

\* \* \*

Let me now briefly present some clinical material from two sessions with my patient Patricia.

> There is a long, bitter silence, full of threats and tension. Then Patricia cries: "I'd like to cut my body to pieces with a pair of scissors!" I remain quiet. After another pause she goes on to say, as if there had been no interruption at all: "... but first I would castrate all men!" (which, of course, includes me too). Again, I am left speechless, my analytic powers castrated.

The second part of Patricia's fantasy provides the explanation to the first. It is because she castrates men in her fantasy, while in reality feeling terrified by them, that Patricia needs the punishment of being cut to pieces. Or is it not the other way around? Is she punishing men in revenge for what they have and she lacks? For the losses which she blames men for: her father, her boyfriend, me? For the "cuts" in herself, in her mind, and in her female body?

Whose body, though? The answer to this question must include an understanding not only of intrinsic bisexuality, whereby Patricia would be using the contemptuous scissors of her aggressiveness to castrate both the female and male parts of herself, but also of the complex and ambiguous nature of her anxiety. Here we can recognise behind the wish to injure the fear of losing control. Behind the dread of sadomasochistic attacks in the future lies the horror of damages that have already taken place in the past. Behind the anxiety of losing and having lost, that of possessing her ambivalently charged phallic scissors.[2]

On another occasion Patricia told me among tears of despair how she experienced her body as being split in two, and how the part from the waist downwards was almost not her own and felt like an intolerable burden. At times that half would move up to her throat and make her feel sick. What I think Patricia was trying to tell me here was that possessing an adult body was causing her a state of such acute anxiety that she could only survive it by regressing to a pregenital form of sexuality and disowning her genital sensations by turning them into an unbearable and sickening burden.

* * *

The phallus, the unconscious representative of the genitals, is distinct from the penis (Birksted-Breen, 1996) and has for each individual, male or female, a variety of meanings. Far from being in all cases or constantly a powerful, damaging weapon of destruction, it can also be a loving object, to be shared with those one cares for, to give oneself and others enjoyment and pleasure. In other words the phallus is often both a weapon through which to express aggressive fantasies and an instrument for communicating loving feelings. When attention is paid only to the latter, anxiety appears to relate to a fear of castration and loss, whereas when both aspects are considered, both castration and possession anxiety emerge as opposite sides of the same complex.

The different, contrasting meanings can switch rapidly back and forth. For instance, a man can experience his penis as a loving object, but suddenly be overwhelmed by aggressive fantasies and withhold it from his sexual partner by becoming impotent; at the same time, by doing so he would also deprive himself of pleasure and thus assuage his guilt about his sadistic fantasies. Or the man suffering from premature ejaculation could experience his penis as a potentially damaging weapon which he is anxious to withdraw as soon as possible from the woman out of love, to protect her from his losing control over it, from ripping her open and destroying her and her contents. The psychology of frigidity could be explained along similar lines, as the woman experiences her own and the male genitals ambivalently, as sources of both pleasure and destruction.

After all, such ambivalence—which is most evident in perversions, for instance sadomasochism, but is fundamentally universal—reflects the common origins of guilt about sexuality in men and women alike. Guilt about getting "too much" pleasure and about conscious or unconscious aggressive fantasies. In both cases the fear of being out of control plays a central role. When we speak of possession anxiety, we should then qualify the term: the anxiety is not so much to do with possessing one's genitals, and all they symbolically represent, but with the use and abuse one could make of them were one to be overwhelmed by instinctual (libidinal or aggressive) wishes and lose control over them.

* * *

I would now like to consider our problem from the viewpoint of its temporal connotations. Hartocollis, who has studied the experience of time as a dimension of affects, believes that "the more one is preoccupied with the future, the more one tends to experience anxiety; and the other way around, the more one feels anxious, the more one worries about the future" (Hartocollis, 1983, p. 107). Although castration anxiety in boys seems to fit this model, being characterised by the anticipation of a dreaded injury and loss in the future, I am not convinced that this applies also to castration anxiety in girls, for whom the injury and loss, so to speak, have already taken place in the past.

Furthermore, what I have termed possession anxiety seems to be present-oriented, with both past and future dimensions colouring the anxiety felt in the present: the past, in so far as the body and the mind we possess now stem from our original endowment and previous experiences; the future, in so far as the present sense of danger has to do, as I have pointed out above, with a fear of a subsequent, yet to happen, and hopefully avoidable loss of control.

Anxiety is related to the expectation of some disastrous event which has not taken place yet. Although, like all affects, it is felt in the present, it requires the potential to conceive of a future perspective that gives to the present feeling its specific quality. This faculty, as we have seen in Chapter One, is not inborn in the child, but acquired as part of the normal development from a primary narcissistic stage of fusion of the self with the outside world (when the infantile omnipresent prevails) to the gradual differentiation of the self from its environment and the establishment of object-relationships.

An important corollary to this formulation is that anxiety, strictly speaking, cannot be experienced from birth, since the mental apparatus has not yet developed the capacity for conceiving of a multidimensional time perspective. More specifically, the origins of possession anxiety, as it should be obvious from what I have outlined so far, should be traced to the genital stage of psychosexual organisation.

> Many years ago a four-year-old girl told me that she knew that there are two differences between the sexes. The first one is

that boys have penises while girls have vaginas; the second one is that boys wear only trousers, while girls can wear either trousers or skirts. She was giving me one straightforward biological fact, to do with anatomy, and another straightforward cultural fact, to do with Western fashion in our time. What is interesting is that she gave them together.

How are we to understand this? Was this child trying to compensate for the anatomical alleged inferiority of girls (penis envy) with their obvious advantage of having available to them a choice of clothing that boys have not? Or was she rather unconsciously suggesting that boys just have a penis (the "trousers") while girls have both a vagina and a penis (the "skirt" and the "trousers"), thus denying her own statement about the first difference between the sexes? This second explanation is supported by the evidence of an episode that took place only a few months later, when that girl had proudly claimed in front of her younger brother, who was playing with his penis after taking a bath, that she had both sexual organs, and proceeded to show him her clitoris.

I think it would be a much reductive interpretation of this material to suggest that the little girl's statements about sexual differences and her exhibitionistic behaviour in front of her brother are motivated only by castration anxiety and penis envy. A theory encompassing an awareness of possessing, and not only of lacking, would do more justice to our child's experience of herself and her body, and to her attempts to explain, in the language characteristic of her age, an otherwise mysterious or unacceptable state of affairs.

What matters to her, in other words, is not just what she lacks (and males, or at least her little brother, have) but also what she has and they have not. Later on this will include the breasts, the womb, and the capacity to generate babies. For the record, this young girl is now a grown-up woman, the mother of two boys.

It is every analyst's clinical experience that people can be as frightened of succeeding—in their relationships, career, therapy—as they can be of failing. Herodotus tells us the story of Polycrates of Samos, a wealthy and successful man who, following the advice of his ally Amasis, Pharaoh of Egypt, tried to get rid of a most precious emerald ring in the hope to avoid having to incur later on Nemesis' wrath and be deprived of all his fortunes; because, the wise king had said, gods allow men to pass through life with alternate success and failure, but never to have an unbroken run of luck without being finally brought to complete ruin. Again, possessing too much luck or prosperity is felt to be a dangerous condition.

Similarly, some people, and dramatic characters such as Shakespeare's Lady Macbeth or Zola's Thérèse Raquin, are wrecked by success and "fall ill precisely when a deeply-rooted and long-cherished wish has come to fulfilment" (Freud, 1916d, p. 316). This Freud attributes to the sense of guilt pertaining to a reactivation in the present of the forbidden triumph originally related to the oedipal situation. Or let us consider the case of a spy coming across a piece of important intelligence, or of a child witnessing intercourse between his parents. Indeed, it must be some anxiety about possessing that information, and not only the fear about having to share it with others and therefore losing it, that turns having a secret into something so dangerous and exciting.

* * *

A specific but significant instance of the two contrasting aspects of anxiety (castration and possession) is the analyst's own emotional attitude towards her patients' analytic material. In the therapeutic process the psychoanalyst should be able to experience, and of course to tolerate, a certain amount of anxiety not only, as it has often been pointed out, about temporarily not knowing and not understanding, but also about getting in touch with, knowing, and understanding the patient's painful memories and feelings. To a lesser extent these faculties should also be available to patients, if they are to meet the demands of psychoanalysis and its setting. Both participants in the analytic situation are likely to have to undergo, and hopefully to survive, anxiety about what makes painful sense and about what makes no sense at all, about what is being discovered or remembered and what is not yet, about words and about silences (see Chapter Nine).

The hypothesis of the presence of another side of the castration complex has implications also for the understanding of the transference. When only castration anxiety is emphasised, the aspect of the transference that tends to be stressed is the patient's worry, which in extreme cases can reach paranoid proportions, that the analyst's interpretations will leave him deprived, empty, fragmented; that analysis will take away his rationality, his sanity, and his power and control over his instinctual drives; that his defences will be crumbled to pieces, leaving him exposed to all sorts of narcissistic traumata; that his sexuality will be turned (will return) to polymorphous perversity and his anger to murderous violence, until his very life will be endangered.

If, on the other hand, the transference relationship is also analysed from the viewpoint of possession anxiety, new constellations will emerge. The focus will be shifted away from the patient's fear of being somehow castrated by his analyst onto his concern about what he could do to the therapist. From a passive experiencing of analysis as a depleting process, the new added perspective on what I call the other side, or the inverse, of the castration complex brings to the fore a more active dimension of the transference, whereby analysands will feel that they have some control over the analytic experience (though of course they might at the same time be worried about losing it). Interpretations will then focus not only on their anxiety about the analyst damaging them, but also on their anxiety about affecting the analyst. By this I do not necessarily mean hurting, raping, murdering, emptying, or devouring her, but also getting close to her, feeding her, loving her, putting the good parts of themselves inside her, sharing what they have, and so on. Or, indeed, they may feel anxious for being unable to do so.

The scope of the analytic process thus widens, the patient becomes a more active participant in it, as Schafer (1983) advocates, the emphasis is shifted from what the patient is anxious about losing or being deprived of, to what he is anxious about, but also maybe proud of, possessing.

* * *

I shall try to illustrate these points with some more clinical material:

> Margaret comments about a plant on my desk which she feels is neglected and in need of support. I say that she often feels neglected and experiences me as being unsupportive. (I have material from many recent sessions with Margaret as evidence for such an interpretation.) She agrees with this, but I am left feeling that she is really only paying lip-service to my words and that my intervention, though correct, is inadequate. She probably experienced it as yet another instance of my being unsupportive to her. I decide to wait and see how the session develops. She soon starts talking about a wish to have me as her guest after the end of her analysis, in order to repay me somehow for what I have been giving her during all these years; I could take whatever I wanted then and she would be listening to me all the time. Then it occurs to her that this is what

she would also like to offer her parents, but she regrets that her house is probably not comfortable enough for them. Margaret then talks about her boyfriend, whom she does not allow herself to love as much as she would like to because she is frightened of becoming too dependent on him. She thinks that it would be nice to take him home to her parents, but she is also concerned that they might disapprove of him or that he might disapprove of them. I suggest that what she really fears is that everybody, including myself, disapproves of her and makes her feel as "neglected and unsupported" as my plant is. After a pause, Margaret expresses concern about an acquaintance who will undergo surgery later that day and may die.

At this point, I remember a dream Margaret had reported the previous week. Its manifest content was that she had been poisoned and as a result was feeling dizzy. Her mother, who was behind a locked door and whom Margaret had asked for help, had replied that there was nothing she could do for her. The associations to the dream had led us to relate it first to a memory of being in a hospital, poisoned with anaesthetics and feeling dizzy, and then to her present anxiety about her boyfriend not being careful enough when they were having sexual intercourse. Margaret had experienced his penis as a poisonous weapon; she was now most worried that she might be pregnant and was constantly watching for signs of pregnancy, such as dizziness. This led her to consider whether she would want to have an abortion.

While thinking back to this dream, a shift occurs in my understanding of the present material, as I become aware of why I have been feeling dissatisfied about my interpretations so far: they now appear to be incomplete because they are dealing with only one side of the conflict Margaret is unconsciously trying to convey to me. I say that she seems to be preoccupied about her frustrated wish to give something to others: support to my plant, hospitality to her parents, listening attention to me, more love to her boyfriend, help to survive surgery to the acquaintance in hospital … In my interpretation I relate Margaret's "maternal" concern to last week's dream: not only to the apparent lack of such concern on the part of her own mother who cannot help her from behind the door, but also to her ambivalent feelings about being pregnant. In particular I suggest that maybe she really wishes to have a baby to whom she could then give all the attention, caring, time, love, and hospitality that she feels filled up with, but unable to offer. The following day Margaret starts the session by saying that she is constipated, which she associates with holding back her feelings.

I hope that this analytic material may show how I attempted to widen the scope of my interpretations by drawing attention to what Margaret possesses (a capacity for concern, for offering hospitality, for looking after, for caring, for feeling worried, for bearing babies), as well as to what she lacks or feels deprived and castrated of (her sense of being neglected, unsupported, inadequate, disapproved of, unlovable). In the course of this session, I had tried to put her in touch not only with the part of herself that identifies with my neglected plant, but also with that part that could look after it.

\* \* \*

Some might object that we can only feel anxious about possessing what we are anxious about losing, and that therefore the concept of possession anxiety is superfluous. But I think that such a view is theoretically and clinically unsatisfactory. It would be analogous to denying sadism (as character trait, as psychological attitude, as sexual perversion) on the grounds that it is nothing but masochism, a manifestation of the death drive, turned outwardly against the object. Or, conversely, to claiming that the concept of masochism is meaningless, being simply a derivative of an aggressive impulse turned inwardly against the self.[3]

\* \* \*

In the final, dramatic lines of *La Roba* (1883), a short story by Giovanni Verga, its protagonist Mazzarò, a landowner who has spent all his miserable life hoarding goods, is told that he is soon to die: it is now time for him to let go of all his earthly possessions and think about his soul. We see him rushing out tottering into the courtyard, hitting and killing his own ducks and turkeys with a stick and shouting like a madman: *"You are my things, you belong to me, come away with me!"*

Possession and castration anxiety, I have suggested, are intimately related. They are two sides of the same coin and they complement each other. Like Mazzarò, we are indeed anxious about losing *and* about possessing all objects we have an ambivalent relationship with. What I am advocating here is not a reformulation of the castration complex, but a shift of emphasis towards the side of it that is usually neglected in psychoanalytic thinking. I am not here too concerned with arguing about which of the two aspects of the castration complex is primary and which secondary, with assessing whether we are mostly anxious about losing what we possess or having what we might lose, with deciding whether our social behaviour is motivated by an intrinsic need for attachment or by a dread of separation, whether it is greed or envy that plays a central role in our attitude towards objects, whether we are dominated by existential angst or by a fear of death. As psycho-analysts we are familiar with primary process functioning and able to conceive of and tolerate contradictions, inconsistencies, and paradoxes. We should know that, much as neurotic symptoms are overdetermined, even simple questions can have more than one answer.

CHAPTER NINE

# Listening to silence

A psychoanalytic session begins with a silence lasting several minutes. Then the patient exclaims: "Unless I can talk to you, *this thing* does not exist!" By "this thing" she means her analysis, our relationship, our presence in my consulting room, here and now. She means her own existence itself: in order for her to feel that she is, the Cartesian *cogitare* is not enough; she needs to be able to verbally *communicate* her thoughts (however painful), her fantasies (however embarrassing), her images (however bizarre).

The silence is broken. "This thing" is allowed to exist.

*   *   *

I am aware of the peculiar dilemma of wishing to write about something (silence), which is by its very nature beyond words, including those that could describe it. I shall restrict myself here to talking about a special form of silence: the one that takes place within that special relationship which is the analytic one. The theme of silence in psychoanalysis has of course been touched upon in many publications and directly approached in several good papers, such as Reik (1926), Fliess (1949), Levy (1958), Arlow (1961), Greenson (1961), Zeligs (1961), Khan (1963), Cremerius (1969), Blos (1972), Green (1979), Leira (1995), Serani

(2000), Ronningstam (2006), Carels (2009), and in a book edited by Nasio (1987).

If psychoanalysis is primarily concerned with the attribution of meaning to our patients' communications, and if we believe silences to be meaningful, it follows that one of our functions as psychoanalysts is to understand the meanings of our patients' silences: learning about their inner worlds involves listening to their silences, not just to their words. Such listening is not a simple operation, as silence often makes others—and psychoanalysts are no exception—feel anxious. As soon as this happens—and until we become aware that it has, and of why—our analytic faculties are impaired. Our efforts are diverted away from our normal capacity to listen in a state of free-floating attention and, before we realise it, we might have become bored and sleepy, or provided inappropriate responses, such as a retaliatory silence or a rushed interpretation.

Silence is often considered to be just a form of resistance to following the "fundamental rule" of psychoanalysis. In early psychoanalytic theory, as Arlow reminds us, "silence was resistance carried to the *nth* degree, since it ran counter to the direction of the therapeutic effort which was to facilitate the flow of accumulated drive cathexes denied discharge by the barrier of repression" (Arlow, 1961, p. 46). But then, of course, in early clinical theory also the transference and the countertransference were just forms of resistance to be overcome. We now know these views to be inadequate for the purpose of understanding what happens in our consulting rooms.

Anna O's definition of the treatment she was receiving from Breuer as "the talking cure" (Freud & Breuer, 1895d) has to this day remained attached to psychoanalysis, and with good reason: communication between analyst and patient takes place mostly through words. "Nothing takes place between them except that they talk to each other," wrote Freud (1926e, p. 187) comparing the tools of the analyst with those of the medical doctor. Pre-verbal and non-verbal expressions, "body language", and acting out are always present and certainly important if we want to understand the full complexity of what our analysands are consciously and unconsciously trying to tell us; yet they are less momentous than words. But what happens *between* words? It should suffice to give a glance to any musical score to realise that rest marks belong to it no less than crotchets and semiquavers. As Beethoven once remarked, "the most important thing in music is not in the score". Reik, in reporting this quotation, comments that, "in psychoanalysis, too, what is spoken is not the most important thing. It appears to us more important to recognize what speech conceals and what silence reveals" (Reik, 1926, p. 186). Without shadows and empty spaces around and between shapes there could be no meaningful representation of form; the exceptions in the work of artists such as M. C. Escher only confirm the rule.

Silence is an element of human language, not its opposite. It is a complement to words, in constant dialectical interaction with them, not their converse. An analytic discourse with no breaks in it would not be a good illustration of the free-associative process, but a parody of it. Besides, is it not conceivable that words too could be used as a form of resistance to getting in touch with something in ourselves that language cannot reach? Should we not allow for, or indeed at times even encourage, such a *silent space* within our patients, ourselves, and the analytic relationship? Should we not tolerate it, listen to it, accept it before, or even instead of, interpreting it, in case it turned out to be a quiet moment of tuning into our patients' internal worlds, an opportunity we are offered to think about them, a chance that would otherwise be missed?

Imagine the following scenario. A patient is on the couch, talking about his depressed mother, authoritarian elder brother, or whatever. You, the analyst, are listening from your armchair, making tentative links in your mind between what your analysand is saying and something else—links that might later lead to an interpretation that you may or may not later suggest to him. There is nothing unusual about any of this. But then, unexpectedly, the patient stops talking, leaving his sentence in mid-air, as if he could not find anywhere the right words to complete it. Or as if, having found them, he could not utter them. Not then-and-there, not to you.

Silence is hanging upon the unfinished. What are you going to do about it? Being a good psychoanalyst, you will probably decide to keep quiet and wait, thinking to yourself about what might have happened. Is your patient's silence related to the content of what he was talking about: his mother, elder brother, or whatever? Is it the result of a sudden intrusion of a disturbing thought, or fantasy, or memory, in his train of associations? Is it a response to something he imagined you were doing, or thinking, or feeling while he was talking? One of these contingencies might strike you, on the basis of your experience and of your deep knowledge of that patient, as being correct, that is, more in tune than others with what you believe is happening in his internal world and in his relationship with you. By this time he might have started talking again, perhaps even commenting upon this very interruption that had caused you to consider what it was all about. Or he might carry on as if no break in his flow of thoughts and words had taken place—a defensive denial on his part, which you may choose to comment about at some point. Or he could resume talking about an apparently unrelated topic, which may again give you some indication of the reasons behind his sudden verbal interruption.

*  *  *

Different silences can have different meanings and they are all richly overdetermined. Silence is not, or not just, an absence (of words), but an active presence.

Freud's (1901b) discovery of the meaningfulness of parapraxes as active processes is relevant to what I am trying to say here. Much as we do not ever lose an umbrella but always leave it behind, and much as we never forget about a dental appointment but "decide" not to remember it, our silences are more than just a lack of verbal expression: they are the result of an active process which, like repression, requires an expenditure of mental energy. We could say, by using a visual image, that silence is like the colour white. Though a white surface appears to be colourless, in fact we know from physics that it consists of the sum total of all colours. This metaphor suggests that we could think of silence as a *container of words*, as a more or less transparent and fragile membrane. The common expression "to break the silence" clearly refers to such a view.

Like the statue that we can paradoxically claim already exists inside the block of marble before the sculptor has touched it with his chisel, words are already there as potentials before being uttered in any interpersonal situation including the psychoanalytic one. Silence can protect words from exposure to hostile treatment (misunderstanding, sarcasm, attacks) or conversely become an impediment to their expression. The safe container becomes a constraint, a prison, a dictatorial regime forbidding the right to free speech. The statue might remain forever buried inside the block of marble.

Silence, then, can be a barrier. It can be a shield. It can be a bridge. It can be a way of avoiding saying something and it can be a way of saying what no words could ever tell. It can express anger, excitement, despair, gratitude, emptiness, joy, shame, helplessness, or indeed any other emotion. I believe that behind all silence there is an unconscious fantasy which the silence, like the dream or the symptom, both conceals and expresses at the same time. A silence during an analytic session could indeed be treated like the manifest content of a dream: we listen to it and then, through our interpretation of the patient's associations, we translate it into the latent wishes, ideas, and fantasies from which it originates. The quality, content, intensity of such wishes, ideas, and fantasies can vary, though ultimately what we are likely to find are their aggressive or sexual components. My point here is an elaboration upon my initial assumption about the meaningfulness of silence. Silence, I am now suggesting, is meaningful and worth being listened to because it is rooted in unconscious fantasies. It is a compromise formation, the end-product of a conflict between different mental agencies, or the result of a tension between different psychic forces that, in the context of the analytic relationship, is experienced within the transference and finds its manifestation as an interruption of the free-associative process. The fundamental rule is broken.

With few exceptions, I would add, most analytic silences stem from a state of unconscious anxiety and often lead to experiencing anxiety in the session. "What is the origin of the uncanny effect of silence, darkness and solitude?" asks Freud (1919h, p. 246). And some pages later he answers: "We can only say that they are actually elements in the production of the infantile anxiety from which the majority of human beings have never become quite free" (Freud, 1919h, p. 252). Perhaps one of the main functions of silence is to transform unconscious anxiety, concerning some as yet unknown or unworked-through inner conflict, into more manageable, though often more painful, conscious anxiety, specifically connected to the analytic relationship.

* * *

Each silence is a pause between two words, two sentences, two discourses. It needs someone who can listen to it and who believes that doing so can enhance the understanding of the silent person's internal world.

My analytic task is to clarify with my patient why she cannot speak to me, rather than trying to make her talk. I have to assess the function of silence for that analysand at that particular moment—the specific unconscious fantasy from which it originates—in order to decide whether or not to interrupt it, and if so, how. Knowing, as Lord Henry does in Oscar Wilde's masterpiece, "the precise psychological moment when to say nothing" (Wilde, 1890, p. 27)—or indeed when to say something—is a difficult task. Our tact, sensitivity, sense of timing, and experience should all be summoned.

As psychoanalysts we have the responsibility of helping our patients to understand not just what they do say, but also why they cannot say that which they are quiet about. Analysands know that all we know about them is what they choose to tell us, even if they often repeat in the transference the childhood illusion that parents know everything about them anyway. Suggesting that we should help our patients to understand why at a particular time they find it impossible to tell us something is another way of stating the importance of the analysis of resistance in our clinical work.

It may be relevant to point out here, by the way, that while all psychoanalytic authors agree that some silences have primarily the function of resistance, they disagree on what other main function they can serve: for instance, Arlow (1961) claims it is "discharge", while Greenson (1961) says it is "communication". I do not see these two positions as mutually exclusive, but I believe that, rather than analysing silence as the result of an economic process involving excessive accumulation of psychic energy and a need to re-establish, through discharge, a balance of forces, it would be more fruitful, both theoretically and clinically, to focus our attention on the meaning of what patients are trying to tell us through their quiet behaviour. In order to understand our analysands' silences and respond to them appropriately, we must take into account some of their specific characteristics. A silence lasting a few seconds, for instance, is intrinsically different from one lasting several minutes. A silence at the beginning of a session is not like one in the middle or towards the end of it. A silence after an interpretation is different from one following the report of a dream. A silence in a patient who is usually talkative is unlike one in someone who is often quiet. A silence in the first session is different from one after years of analysis.

Rather than concentrating on the technical aspects of how to assess and deal with these different silences, I shall emphasise here that if we consider silence as part of the communication between patient and analyst we cannot focus our attention only on "silent patients"—a shorthand expression for "patients who are silent at a particular time, and for particular reasons"; we must also look at the function of silence in the therapist.

> Joanna felt empty inside, filled with a great void. Her long silences in the sessions were its external manifestation, indeed its language. My silences were to her confirmation of that void. There was noth-ing for me to say to her, because there was nothing inside her that I, or anybody else, could have said anything about. At times, when she felt less depressed, Joanna wondered about what I might have been feeling while she was silent on the couch: was I thinking about her? Was I trying to guess at what was going through her mind? Was I thinking about my own business? But then she would con-clude: "We don't speak to each other. It is all my fault. Everything must be just a big void."

How does the silence of the analyst interact with that of the analysand? Silence, I have noted, is part of communication, and as such it can take place only within a relationship: it is an interpersonal phenomenon. The silence of the analyst is not a silence at all if the patient is talking. The silence of the patient is not a silence at all either if the analyst is talking.

But when neither is talking who is being silent? The words and the silences of the patient, whatever their content and meaning, are different from the words and the silences of the analyst because psy-choanalysis is primarily a monologue and not a dialogue. The relevant questions to ask here are whether the silence of the analyst will sup-port or disturb that of the patient, whether it will interfere with it or complement it.

> Hilary needed several minutes of silence as she lay down on the couch before being able to feel settled and to talk. Neither of us spoke. I became convinced that she was using the first few moments of her sessions not only to prepare herself for free asso-ciating, but also as a kind of "dustbin" where she could silently dispose of unacceptable thoughts and feelings, which could then be left unanalysed. I had to wait patiently for the appropriate time to suggest this interpretation. For the first few years doing so only made Hilary more defensive—and more silent.
>
> Olga's silences often created for me a serious technical problem. I knew that she was likely to experience my letting her stay quiet

as evidence of my lack of understanding and caring. At the same time I also knew that she would have experienced my breaking her silence as a painful and persecutory intrusion into her space. Pointing out my dilemma to Olga was at times the only way to break through this impasse.

This dilemma in the analyst is only one side of the wider paradoxical predicament that the chronically silent patient poses, a predicament that can be seen as paradigmatic of the analytic relationship as a whole. The analysand lying quiet on my couch, whatever the meaning of his particular silence, is indicating that he is with me *to tell me that he cannot tell me anything*—which is not a meaningless statement.

* * *

Let us go back to the analyst's silence. Is it going to be liberating or persecutory? A sign of respect for the patient's space and time, whose boundaries should not be trespassed, or a demonstration of how cold, uncaring, and aggressive we can be, under the guise of our "neutral" technique, of "therapeutic" distance, of "surgical" interventions, of "reflective" mirrors, and the like? At times we feel a need, almost an urge, to fill the vacuum, to say something without quite knowing what to say. The content escapes us. We look for it in vain among the infinite number of possible combinations of phonemes and find but meaningless words, incompletable sentences, commonplaces, or stupid remarks. And yet that need to actively intervene has the strength of real necessity. To be quiet, at that point, is a mistake, though to speak without knowing what to say can only be another mistake: "What we cannot speak about we must pass over in silence" is Wittgenstein's (1922, p. 74) unequivocal instruction. We can only wait, then, fettered to our mute discomfort, while knowing that the longer our silence goes on the harder it will be to break it. Time tends to toughen the membrane of the container.

Our art consists in the capacity to express, as well as to understand, what is near the boundaries of decency, of the shameful, of the unspeakable; what belongs to us and to everyone but is hidden in an almost unreachable territory, yet close. At times, like Poe's "purloined letter" (Poe, 1845), invisible because too obviosly displayed, unavailable because too close.

* * *

A patient's silence might be a form of protesting the analyst's fundamental rule, a resistance to her as a person, to her setting, and to the therapeutic process as a whole. To this an analyst might be unable—because of her own intolerance, anxiety, psychopathology, or countertransference difficulties—to respond appropriately.

The analyst might, for instance, become excessively silent herself, through identification with the patient. This is likely to be experienced by the latter as persecutory, rejecting, or punitive. The analyst, having become a wall of silence, is no longer performing her therapeutic role, not even as a reflecting mirror. At the opposite end of the spectrum, the analyst, possibly through guilt, can become over-interpretative, flooding her quiet patient with words. This reminds me of a tragic episode in contemporary history: some American soldiers who entered Nazi extermination camps in 1945 were so overwhelmed by the state in which they found the starving survivors that they overfed them, thus unwittingly causing their death (Gilbert, 1987, pp. 809–810).

If words are comparable to food because of their oral connotations and the enriching, nourishing function they can have, silence, then, especially if prolonged and repeated, can at times be equated to a form of symbolic anorexia: where both the patient and the analyst (like the anorexic girl and her mother) are kept emotionally starving.

> Paul almost invariably stopped talking five to ten minutes before the end of each session: he was terrified of being caught unawares when I announced that time was up. The final part of practically all his sessions was spent in a state of anxious silence, though he ignored how long this would last, as he never wore a watch. What if I did interrupt him while he was in the middle of telling me something important? What if I did not interrupt him and let him go on beyond his allotted fifty minutes, and he later found out that he had deprived me of a few moments of my precious time? This was eventually related to oral issues as we discovered how frightened he was to appear too needy and greedy: through his silence, Paul left the last crumbs of food on the plate, so that I should not know how hungry he still really felt.

Several authors, notably Ferenczi (1916–17) and Abraham (1919), have emphasised the anal-retentive quality of silence. If "the function of speech is not only communicative but serves also to discharge instinctual feelings … [then] silence represents an unconscious defense against the discharge of such conflictual feelings … a form of sphincter closure, displaced from the original erotogenic zones to the organs and functions of speech, in order to maintain repression of pregenital impulses" (Zeligs, 1961, p. 13). It is no coincidence that, in common language, logorrhoea is often described as verbal diarrhoea and silence is considered to be "golden". When words are symbolically associated with faeces, silence becomes the expression of constipation. A silence displaying such anal connotations would be characterised by an ambivalent, if not openly aggressive, attitude. This quality, of course, is typical of compulsive symptoms, which represent in their structure and function the conflict between two contrasting impulses: the patient is at the same time trying to express his forbidden thoughts (Ferenczi's "obscene words", 1911) and to repress them.

Partly following the important work of Robert Fliess (1949) who differentiates all silences as being oral, anal, or urethral, we could then also postulate the existence of a "phallic" silence. Words can be experienced as an extension of the body, as well as of the psyche, with the capacity to penetrate the ears and minds of the listener. Language itself is often eroticised and used for seductive (active or passive) purposes. In this sense, then, silence is unconsciously associated with phallic impotence and can become a defence against castration and possession anxieties pertaining to this stage of development (see Chapter Eight). Keeping quiet is a way of protecting the parents, the analyst, and oneself, from exposure to the dangers of sexuality, aggression, and retaliation that characterise the Oedipus complex. Silence becomes a sort of self-censorship, in order to reassure oneself that one will not say anything wrong. It may be noted here that in democratic societies people under arrest have a legal right to keep silent.

We further find a symbolic equation of language with the act of procreation. Words, spoken or written, can be felt at times as the babies we create and nourish and love. The "pregnant" silence preceding them—the quiet before the storm, the still unpainted canvas on the artist's easel, the white sheet of paper on the writer's desk—could then be experienced as a time of preparation for creative activity. The inner void is being filled; silence is related to hope in the future and to the expectation of new life.

In contrast to this optimistic interpretation, countless poets, not just psychoanalysts, have postulated a symbolic link between silence and death. Silence can express the loss of an object, a loss which can be real or imagined, experienced in the past or anticipated in the future. Those in mourning (who suffer in silence) withdraw from the dead (who do not speak) not just affects but also the words that belong to them. Affects and words, which (to use Freud's economic model) are then re-cathected, as depression and silence respectively, onto the self. We have already observed in Chapter Three the important role played by silence in the analysis of Renate, who experienced every silence, whether in her social life or in her analysis, as a paralysing situation for which she felt responsible.

> Dennis, another patient, became very upset if I kept silent for more than a few moments. He needed to frequently hear my words in order to reassure himself that I had been listening to him and that I could respond appropriately to what he had said. This need was the manifestation of a fear that he and I might die or become mad in the course of the session as a result of his expressing aggressive and destructive wishes. As long as we both talked, and could prove through our words that we could understand and communicate with each other, Dennis could trust that both of us were still alive and sane.

It is the silent universe of self-blinded Oedipus—the tragic persona-lisation of our human condition of ultimate loneliness—in his and our wanderings through life, that has to be avoided at all costs, which means by using all available defences: an anguish that cannot be put into words because there is nothing, or perhaps too much, to be said about it. In these instances the silent patient appears as a person who is mourning the loss of his analyst. His silence can be a memory, a repetition, or an anticipation of an analytic break—or indeed of any separation from any object—and can have the positive function of mourning a past or present loss, or of anticipatory grief of a future one: "The rest is silence", are Hamlet's last words before expiring.

We know that, however real such an experience can feel to the analysand, what is lost is mostly not the analyst as a person, or even as the symbol of the psychoanalytic process in which the trust is faltering, but whoever the analyst is representing to the patient in the transference. The loss, experienced in the here-and-now of the analytic session as the present loss of a real object, and expressed through a silent response to the therapist, is a past loss of a transference object, and as such should be understood and interpreted.

"The magnificence of silence in interpersonal relationships", writes Arlow, "is its very ambiguity … In the transference situation the ambiguity of silence affords the patient an opportunity to invite the analyst to share his fantasy-emotions" (Arlow, 1961, p. 51). We should accept this invitation and make the most of it.

\* \* \*

The unconscious is timeless. The unconscious is silent.

Before *in principio* (before time), before the *verbum* (before word-presentation), there was an all-encompassing silence, ontogenetically repeated in all human earliest experiences: "Silence", writes Cremerius, "is the form of communication characterizing primitive mother infant relationships at the stage of subject and object fusion" (Cremerius, 1969). At the breast, the dialogue between mother and baby is mostly a silent one. That primitive timelessness which I have described as infantile omnipresent has no words. And yet, "no words" does not mean silence. The infant in his mother's arms—and earlier the foetus in her womb—is immersed in a universe of sounds. Some even argue that the infant's earliest and most important experiences are auditory in nature: "The sound space is the first psychical space" (Anzieu, 1985, p. 170). In the absence of words, sounds and noises become more charged with meanings. At night, a child can be terrified by the cracking noise of furniture, or else reassured by the familiar sound of water running from the kitchen tap, which he would hardly bother to listen for in daytime while playing with a friend.

In some psychoanalytic sessions silence as a preverbal form of communication can be a way of regressing to a safer space, which might resemble in fantasy the womb, the cot, or sleep. If the analyst then respects the patient's silence—if she empathically understands it and is capable of responding to it appropriately, either through good interpretations or through her own silence—the couch can become such a safe space, and analysis an emotionally enriching experience.

\* \* \*

It would be easy now to point out the contradictions contained in this chapter. I have suggested that silence is unconsciously related to the void, to nothingness, to fear of death and annihilation, and is ultimately connected with deep-rooted anxiety. And yet I have also said that it is full of overdetermined, rich significance, and that it can express any feelings, including joy, excitement and gratitude. I have said that silence is a bridge and I have said it is a container. That it is a shield and that it is an intrinsic element of all verbal exchanges. I have said that, being related to a preverbal form of communication, it characterises regression, but I have also implied that not saying what cannot be talked about is at times the most mature thing to do. I have described silence as a form of verbal anorexia, verbal constipation, verbal impotence, and verbal pregnancy.

If then, as it seems, I have presented a picture that is so full of contradictory statements or suggestions, am I not leaving my readers, and indeed myself, more confused than before I started? I hope not. I am convinced that in order to examine a phenomenon which has the complexity, the richness, the mystery of silence we must dissect it into its components, focus upon various of its features and be prepared to change perspectives of observation. If this leads to contradictions and paradoxes, we must stay with them a little longer. Perhaps staying with our patients' and our own silences a little longer is the one unambiguous recommendation I can honestly make about this subject.

## CHAPTER TEN

# Listening to sounds

*"What passion cannot music raise and quell?"*

—John Dryden, *A Song for St Cecilia's Day*, 1687

There are some similarities between music and psychoanalysis. First of all, they are both exquisitely auditory experiences and both require interpretations in order to come alive. Furthermore, the idiom we use in relation to musical form can also be profitably applied to the therapeutic process. We can think of the psychoanalytic encounter itself in musical terms, with its specific melodic, harmonic and rhythmical patterns, its *crescendos* and *diminuendos* of emotional tension, at a *largo* tempo with some patients or at a more frantic *allegro vivace* with others. Some sessions may be described as presenting an initial theme followed by variations, others in terms of their chromatic or diatonic quality, in a confident major key or in a depressive minor one, and so on *ad lib*. The auditory apparatus is at the core of both psychoanalytic and musical listening even if, to be fair, not all of our patients' utterances, or indeed our own, sound particularly musical! The tone of the therapist's voice, as well as the timing of her interventions, is often as important as her words. And silences in analytic sessions can be as intensely charged with meaning (see Chapter Nine) as the dynamic indication *niente* (nothing) in some scores is charged with sound, for example, in the last bars of Vaughan Williams's *Dona Nobis Pacem* (1936, p. 68).

Other similarities can be found between music and the structure of the psychoanalytic setting. One of my patients described the beginning of each session as a kind of ballet routine—I open the door, she walks in, I close the door, she lies down, I sit down, she starts talking, etc.—more or less identically repeated day in, day out; year in, year out. Freud (1913c) had recognised something similar when, using a different metaphor, he had compared the beginning of analysis to the predictable opening moves of a game of chess. More generally, the psychoanalytic setting discourages tactile and visual interchange, with the analyst sitting out of sight of the patient who is lying on the couch, and favours verbal communication instead, that is the establishment of an auditory experience through the expectation of free associations from the patient and free-floating attention in the therapist—the equivalent, by the way, of the "stream of consciousness" in literature (*e.g.*, Virginia Woolf) and of improvisation in music (*e.g.*, jazz).

Last but not least, music should be of interest to psychoanalysts because of its powerful effect on our emotional life and even on our behaviour: "Music oft hath such a charm / To make bad good and good provoke to harm" (Shakespeare, *Measure for Measure*, IV, i, 14).

\* \* \*

Sigmund Freud intended psychoanalysis to be not only a form of therapy for the relief of emotional suffering and an instrument of clinical investigation into the deepest recesses of the mind, but also a general psychology which could provide interpretations to such disparate phenomena as jokes, parapraxes, group dynamics, and artistic production. He demonstrated through his own writings that the psychoanalytic method could be successfully applied to social anthropology, mythology, history of religion, biography, and, last but not least, literary and art criticism. In approaching the subject of the relationship of psychoanalysis to music, we would then want to refer back to Freud himself. We shall, however, be disappointed: "Freud's aversion to music", Jones informs us, "was one of his well-known characteristics" (Jones, 1953, p. 20). The founder of psychoanalysis never published anything on music, and he openly admitted his indifference to it. In the first page of his essay on Michelangelo's statue of Moses (Freud, 1914b, p. 211) he claims that although "works of art do exercise a powerful effect on me ... I am almost incapable of obtaining any pleasure [from music]" and in a letter to Marie Bonaparte (6 December, 1936; quoted in Jones, 1957, p. 226) he describes himself as "quite unmusical" ("*ganz unmusikalischer Mensch*"). Some seventy years earlier, young Sigmund had convinced his mother to remove a piano from the flat, thus putting an end to his eight-year-old sister Anna's musical education, on the grounds that her practising disturbed his studies (Jones, 1953, p. 20). If we ignore the speculations of some researchers (*e.g.*, Diaz de Chumaceiro, 1992; 1993), all the evidence available to Freud's biographers suggests that his contacts with music were limited to a superficial knowledge and appreciation of a handful of operas—notably *Don Giovanni* but also *Le nozze di Figaro, Die Meistersinger* and *Carmen*—and even then more because of their visual and narrative components than because of their music (Gay, 1988, pp. 168–169). Librettist Da Ponte intrigued him more than composer Mozart. And it is of little satisfaction for a Freudian to learn that the only reference to music in Jung's autobiography is to the "polyphony" created by the water boiling in a large kettle (Jung, 1961, pp. 256–257).

Freud's "aversion" and ignorance in this field are remarkable in view of the fact that his mother was apparently very musical, his brother Alexander "could whistle in perfect tune a whole opera" (M. Freud, 1957, p. 17), and Sigmund himself had multiple and direct exposures to the musical world. Vienna, with a classical tradition including the likes of Haydn, Mozart and Schubert, was still in his days the capital of music, home to illustrious guests such as Bruckner, Brahms, and Mahler, as well as to avant-garde composers Schoenberg, Berg, and Webern. The most popular musicians in town, however, were then Johann Strauss and his waltzing relatives—who, it was half-jokingly said, were helping the Viennese to forget, while Freud was helping them to remember. One of Freud's close associates and a founding member of his Psychological Wednesday Society (the informal group started in 1901 which became in 1908 the Vienna Psycho-Analytical Society) was the eminent musicologist Max Graf (see Abrams, 1993). According to him, "Freud himself was not musical, which he regretted ... [but] welcomed conversations with a musician, which gave him access to a field unfamiliar to him" (Graf, 1957, p. 163). Graf's son Herbert, the "Little Hans" in Freud's

(1909) celebrated case of a phobic child, was to become a prominent operatic stage designer.

Freud had also had brief but intense professional contacts with Bruno Walter and Gustav Mahler. Their meetings are well documented and worth reporting. In 1904 Walter, then Mahler's young assistant conductor at the Vienna Court Opera, was afflicted by a mysterious paralysis to his right arm for which he eventually consulted Freud. Walter expected to be questioned about his childhood sexuality but, much to his surprise, he had his arm examined and was then advised to leave straightaway for a holiday in Sicily. Upon Walter's return to Vienna, the problem not having subsided, Freud saw the musician a few more times, when he instructed him to forget about his problem (à la Strauss!) and go back to conducting. In his autobiography, Walter recalls the ensuing exchange with his analyst: "'But I can't move my arm.' 'Try anyway.' 'And if I have to stop?' 'You won't!' 'How could I face being responsible for a possible interruption in the performance?' 'I will take that responsibility upon myself.'" (Walter, 1947, p. 184). Gradually, by trying to "forget" about his arm, Walter overcame his paralysis—a most unorthodox but apparently successful therapeutic intervention.

As to Gustav Mahler, Freud analysed the composer's anxiety concerning his troubled relationship with his wife Alma in a long single session in August 1910 in Leyden (Holland), during a holiday. At the end of the momentous meeting, Freud felt about his understanding of the musician's internal world that "it was as if a single ray of light could penetrate through a mysterious edifice" (Freud, in a letter of 1935 to Theodor Reik; in Reik, 1953, p. 343).

Whatever the overdetermined reasons for Freud's almost exaggerated—and therefore perhaps suspect ("this is not the full story ..." suggests Jones [1953, p. 20]; see also Cheshire, 1996)—indifference, ambivalence, or even hostility towards music, many psychoanalysts past and present have been involved with music personally, and sometimes professionally. A number of them may only be regular concert-goers, or just the owners of enviable compact disc collections, but some also have a sophisticated knowledge of musical theory and history, or are even fine performers themselves. Yet, even they tend to keep their interest, or passion, for music and for psychoanalysis in two separate compartments, arguing that music, the purest and most abstract of all arts, ultimately belongs to an almost sacred, non-verbal (or pre-verbal) universe where it should be enjoyed and left alone. A colleague I often meet at concerts once told me: "I already spend my whole day putting what I hear into words and I don't want to have to do the same with music." I am in some sympathy with his position and believe that it is legitimate to question the desirability of using words to explain our musical experiences. However, assuming that we want not only to enjoy music but also to understand why we do, what else could we use? Is it not one of our analytic tasks to lend words to phenomena placed "beyond words"?

* * *

I will not indulge here on biographical, or pathographical, studies of composers: I will refrain from speculating on the vicissitudes of the internalised paternal imago of Leopold Mozart in his son's productions, or on the erotisation of Wagner's relationship to his mother as represented in his use of the *leitmotiv*—to take two examples from musicians not unfamiliar to Freud. Nor will I even attempt, with the help of psychoanalytic interpretative instruments, a critical analysis of musical compositions, say of one movement of a piano sonata, by attributing the meaning of repression into the unconscious to its numerous descending scale passages; by understanding a haunting phrase as the representation of the demands of a harsh superego by comparing the harmonic structure of its finale to the resolution of a preoedipal conflict, etcetera. It is my impression that such intellectual exercises, whenever tried before, have given disappointingly sterile results.

Rather, I will start by asking an impossible question. Is musical, or for that matter any artistic talent, innate or is it acquired? Are "quite unmusical" individuals like Freud people who are not given (by parents, educators, prevailing cultural values) the opportunity to develop qualities they possess? "Despite the widespread acceptance of the idea that only certain people are born to be musical, the notion that everyone is musical is probably closer to the true situation," write Sloboda, Davidson and Howe. (1994). And even if we agree that some people have a better innate disposition to musicality (whatever we mean by that elusive word), we must still consider which part early individual auditory experiences have played in its establishment. This is what I shall examine here with reference to psychoanalytic theories of child development.

* * *

I will leave it to others (*e.g.*, Piontelli, 1992) to observe and speculate on what happens to foetuses inside the womb in relation to their perception and experience of sounds, such as the rhythmical thumping of the mother's heart. As suggested in Chapter One, at birth instincts and their gratifications form a unit, the self is narcissistically omnipotent, with no clear sense of identity: subject and object are an inseparable whole. As a result, the baby cannot yet recognise the possibility of interpersonal relationships. It may be noted here that a component in the adult listener's ecstatic enjoyment of music in a concert hall may consist of a "regression in the service of the ego" (Kris, 1952) to such a primitive undifferentiated state; to a momentary loss of the sense of time, of space, and of personal identity; to an "oceanic" fusion between himself and the outside world. Listeners let their affects flow while at the same time remaining in control over them (Salomonsson, 1989) in a complex marriage "of primary process imaginative freedom with secondary process logical control" (Rose, 1992, p. xx).

Experiences of close contact between babies and their caring parents are of fundamental importance. As to the role of sounds and familiar voices during the earliest phases of human life, all goes back, in Rose's colourful image, to "Opus N° 1, the first duet" (Rose, 1993, p. 78) between mother and baby. Infant feeding as the prototype of nourishing interchanges and of later intimacy involves tactile, olfactory, visual, and auditory contacts—the sounds produced by the suckling child and by mother's voice in their quiet dialogues at the breast—to which we know babies to be very sensitive. "Since the infant still lacks the capacity of relating to language as a semantic system", writes Noy, "he is indeed responding merely to the various sound components—intensity, pitch, rhythm and timbre" (Noy, 1968, p. 65), to which adults intuitively and universally contribute by speaking or sing-songing to young children in a high and modulated pitch. Storr points out that music derives from an "emotional need for communication with other human beings which is prior to the need for conveying objective information or exchanging ideas" (Storr, 1992, p. 16). From the perspective of the child, nothing could then be further from the truth than the statement that children "should be seen and not heard". In fact, the need to be heard is vital also within adult relationships. Many of us feel invalidated or annihilated in our sense of identity when our voices and words and sounds are being ignored. The narcissistic wound resulting from this distressing experience can feel unbearable and lead to either intense depression, or blind (or should I say deaf) rage. In this sense, one may wonder whether musicians are people particularly sensitive to the need of making themselves heard by others. We may also remember that the experience of being heard, in the deepest meaning of the word, constitutes one of the main therapeutic factors in psychoanalysis. The so-called "talking cure" is primarily a "listening cure".

* * *

Let us go back to the nursery. Silent feeding sessions with a mother never addressing sounds or words to her baby may be distressing for the child, and could amount to perceptual and emotional deprivation, possibly causing future problems in the development of linguistic and musical skills, or to overt psychopathology. In so far as early auditory experiences are then crucial to the establishment of a sense of self, deaf babies will have difficulties in the process of psychological individuation, though the potential handicap may be partly offset by compensatory mechanisms such as hyper-perceptivity in other sensory modalities (the reason why some blind people are excellent piano tuners). If early eye contact with objects at close distance provides a prototype of visual experiences, leading to the structuring of spatial coordinates (Wright, 1991), voice contact linking objects at earshot (possibly placed then outside each other's visual field) provides a prototype of auditory experiences, leading to the structuring of temporal coordinates. In this connection, music "is the art of time par excellence" (Rose, 1992, p. 156), it is "time made audible" (Langer, 1957, p. 38).

* * *

In order to survive the inevitable delays in the gratification of the child's needs, her psychic apparatus must develop the capacity to tolerate the resulting frustrations. The delicate transition from the original state of fusion with the primary object to the subsequent stage of relative separation from it is made possible by the emerging capacity to imagine objects in one's mind. When the object is absent the child has to use her newly acquired mastery of space and time—obtained through early tactile, olfactory, visual, and auditory contacts with the world—in order to recreate in her mind the missing gratifying object. This recreation is in fact a new creation. Coloured by the child's own fantasy, a new internal world is invented and begins to take its own original shape. Her acquisition of a mental understanding of the world is then a gradual achievement, which takes time and often causes much suffering, though it can also be exciting: indeed, one of the pleasures in life is to find, or perhaps to re-find, lost objects. To re-find old objects in newly created ones might be a good description of the driving force behind all later scientific endeavours and artistic activities.

Psychological growth also requires mirroring. The child "finds" himself in the eyes of his mother; he begins to recognise his separate identity in the positive image reflected by the parental gaze. I would like to suggest here that another aspect of mirroring, in parallel to the visual one described by Winnicott (1967), concerns the reflection of the child's voice, sounds, and noises—a process I here propose to call "echoing" (see also Anzieu, 1985, pp. 170–74). Such holding auditory reflection will eventually allow the child not just to produce sounds for which he is already endowed at birth with a suitable anatomo-physiological apparatus, but also to learn to listen to them, enjoy them, and recognise them as his own. For echoing to take place, the empathic and containing voice of his carers is an indispensable sounding-board, or resonance box, to the child's voice. Only by being talked and listened to by those who love him, will the child feel sufficiently supported to learn to listen to himself (literally and metaphorically) and thus gradually develop an individual identity. I believe that this will also prove to be a crucial factor in his capacity for a future appreciation, or even performance or composition, of music. Let me note here, by the way, that listening to one's own voice within a holding environment is what characterises the psychoanalytic experience itself. Finally, those objects which Winnicott (1953) calls transitional, situated as they are at the interface between fantasy and reality, have here an important role. There is evidence (McDonald, 1970; Oremland, 1975) that mentally or vocally repeated familiar tunes have for most young children a considerable part to play as transitional musical experiences, belonging both to the child's own self and to her external world, and facilitating a satisfactory relationship between the two. Again, the absence of such experiences, as may be the case with autistic children, could be a symptom of current or future psychological impairment.

* * *

The gradual acquisition of a sense of identity, here delineated in its main features, culminates during what Mahler, Pine and Bergman (1975) describe as the separation–individuation stage: the child begins to move away physically (by learning to crawl and then walk) and psychologically from his parents. Ultimately, though, no one entirely succeeds: throughout life human beings return "home", wherever that may be, for emotional refuelling. For toddlers who are learning to gradually move away from their parents and to negotiate a tolerable distance from them, sounds and voices can represent a link with the safe environment that they are temporarily leaving behind in search of their own individuality and autonomy—a search that will continue, with different modalities and varying degrees of success, for the rest of their lives. "The use of music and sound in extending the link from mother to child is a core issue in the move towards differentiation and in the development of a sense of reality" (Nass, 1984, p. 483). If the "echoing" of such familiar sounds and voices is missing, the child may be thrown into a frighteningly empty universe of silence where she will feel insecure and therefore unable to safely move forward towards independence.

* * *

It should be apparent from the above considerations that the relationship between psychoanalysis and music is a complex, multifaceted one which should be approached from a variety of different angles. On the one hand, music might contribute original interpretations to some features of psychological life: "Acoustic-musical experience and expression occupy an exceptional position in relation to other sensory modalities. Consequently, musical creations may be a primary source for insights into certain aspects of psychic functioning" (Feder, Karmel & Pollock, 1990, pp. xiv–xv). On the other hand, psychoanalysis has the instruments to allow us to understand many features of the musical idiom. In recent years analysts have begun to explore such areas as the relationship between music and affects, the psychogenetics of musical experience, the links between the development of verbal, mathematical and musical languages, as well as the origins, structure and significance of creativity in relation to music. It is true that, if compared to the richness of psychoanalytic writings on literature, theatre, films, or visual arts (or indeed with the vast body of psychological research on music [Sloboda, 1985]) psychoanalytic inquiries in this field are still scanty.[1] The complex cultural connections between psychoanalysis and music have not yet received thorough critical examination, and opportunities for cross-fertilisation have been missed. Yet psychoanalysis as a developmental psychology could provide a theoretical basis for the clarification of many aspects of music. Future research in this field could be crucial to an understanding of the origins of early sensory experiences and object-relationships, as well as of the child's appreciation of the world of sounds, which may later develop into specific musical sensitivities. It is hoped that musicians and musicologists with an interest in psycho-analytic ideas, and analysts with a passion for music, may find further explorations in this areas to bear fruitful results.

## CHAPTER ELEVEN

# In between and across

*We build too many walls and not enough bridges.*

—Sir Isaac Newton

Margins, borders, frames, edges, thresholds, and boundaries ... Empty spaces, grey areas, anti-chambers, half-way houses, and no-man's lands ... Links, bonds, ties, zips, hinges, and bridges ...

Intrigued by the power of words to evoke and provoke, to hurt and heal, to embarrass and inspire, I propose for this chapter a topic which, by its ambiguous or even paradoxical nature, seems almost unapproachable. This is because it covers psychological and cultural domains which, while universally observable, only exist in a state of permanent potentiality, or of dynamic impermanence, located as they are in between and across other more clearly identifiable territories. They border on these, and share with them certain features, but in fact they do not belong anywhere tangible. And, if they don't really exist, they must also be beyond words ... I will nevertheless try to use my own words to give at least a flavour of this subject. I'll endeavour to do so by referring to some of its manifestations, arbitrarily selected from different fields.

The theoretical underpinning to my considerations originates in Donald W. Winnicott's transitional space, described by him as a sort of playground or "resting-place for the individual engaged in the perpetual human task of keeping inner and outer reality separate yet interrelated" (Winnicott, 1953, p. 230). This is an area of fantasy, play, and creativity placed somewhere between the self and the external world.

Here I intend to expand on that original concept in two important directions. The first involves the introduction of the dimension of time, to be added to that of space, thus focusing our attention not just on the spatial distance (*"Neither here nor there"*) but also on the experience of the temporal interval (*"No longer this, but not yet that"*) between two events. In other words, as well as speaking of a transitional space it would be useful also to consider the existence of a *transitional time*—one can think here about those moments of dawn and twilight when day and night dissolve into each other. What happens between two events: for instance, after we have offered a patient an interpretation and before she responds to it? What happens between two states of mind: for instance, passing out and regaining consciousness, rational reasoning and psychotic delusion, feeling contented and becoming enraged (and back again)? What happens in the brief moment when, still half-asleep, your hand switches off the alarm clock on the bedside table, while the rest of you emerges from the fantastical sureality of a dream?

My second extension of Winnicott's idea concerns the introduction of the concept of a *spatio-temporal bridge*—a bridge being a structure spanning an obstacle for the purpose of providing passage over it. While the transitional space relates to the potential area between two objects (to use Winnicott's own colourful expression in relation to toddlers, "between the thumb and the teddy bear" [1953, p. 2]) and implies a developmental movement from one towards the other (*e.g.*, from a mainly narcissistic investment in one's own body towards whole object-relationships with other human beings), my metaphor of the spatio-temporal bridge also implies that, in the process of connecting two separate objects, events, or mental states, we can imagine something extending over and above what lies between them. A crossing over that may remind us of Coleridge's "suspension of disbelief", that aspect of illusion as necessary to, say, the audience in a concert hall, as it is to psychoanalysts listening to their patients.

A helpful image bridging over both space and time is that of the *journey*, a metaphor for psychoanalysis ("trips through transference country", in Roy Schafer's words [1983, p. 259]) and indeed for life itself, in the sense of travel that almost disregards the departure and arrival points. By carrying people in their journeys from A to B, ships and trains and other assorted vehicles perform an obvious bridging function. Intriguing among them, and invested with almost mythical qualities, are those occasional semi-public means of transportation known in most languages as taxis. Black in London, white in Milan, yellow in New York, they are integral, symbolic elements of our urban landscapes. As they flash past us in the streets having just picked up or delivered their customers, taxis are impermanent and anonymous entities. Taxis are self-contained islands; they are bridges; they are ambiguously connotated transitional spaces and times—womb-like cocoons protecting us from the external world while at the same time exposing us to mortal dangers. Iconic containers-on-wheels of fears and desires, of assorted luggage and hopes and dreams, taxis seem to exist only to remind us that, whether happily rolling along a tree-lined avenue or stuck in a traffic jam, we are ultimately alone in our existential journeys.

* * *

The spatio-temporal bridge image seems particularly apt to describe cultural activities. For instance, in the case of cinema, we could say that pictures as well as linking the filmmaker's fantasies to those of the spectators, and the fantasies of both to objective reality, also imaginatively cross over the everyday experience of the external world, while at the same time placing their very foundations in it.

In considering psychological and cultural phenomena from this perspective it is helpful to keep in mind the distinction, sometimes almost imperceptible, between what separates different elements and prevents communication between them (such as censorship, brickwalls, checkpoints, fences and barriers) and what, instead, holds these parts together and facilitates exchange between them: links, interfaces, hinges, joints, and more or less permeable filters. A paradigmatic instance here is the image of a baby in a double-bed, peacefully asleep between her parents: joining them together in their love for her, yet also keeping them apart.

That same front door of my house serves the double function of keeping intruders away and of welcoming friends in. It is interesting to note how the balance between these two functions of doors differs in different societies. In rural environments, in many communities, and in certain countries even in urban centres, doors are normally left unlocked, thus suggesting that people lack there the suspiciousness of one another that characterises the attitude of all those who would always lock their front door. But it is not just a question of trust in one's neighbours; those whose behaviour in this respect indicates the importance of "letting their friends in" as opposed to "keeping their enemies out", I suggest, may have an altogether different approach to boundaries—in their interpersonal relationships, in their attitude towards their environment, in their perception of space and time, and of the "bridges" connecting different aspects of their experiences and of their internal world.

* * *

As we have seen in Chapter Three, when discussing the issue of virginity, a girl may experience her genitals as a closed door or as an open window of opportunities. Adolescence as a whole, perhaps more so than other life stages, can be viewed in terms of the transitional time it occupies in a person's existence, and as such it is marked in many societies by specific rites of passage (such as in the Jewish tradition of Bar Mitzvah). It is a time often experienced by young individuals, whose bodies are not yet fully grown, with considerable confusion, as childish needs clash with adult strivings. Italians commonly refer to adolescents going through this stage with the rather crude expression, *"Né carne, né pesce"* ("Neither meat, nor fish").

An exceptional instance of temporal transition, as we have seen in Chapter Six, was the approaching beginning of the third millennium, a collective event marked by countless rites of passage. In my speculations about the fantasies attached to that symbolic watershed I reasoned that there seemed to be something narcissistically gratifying about belonging to a generation that stretched across two millennia.

At a more personal level, all sorts of rites of passage, from baptisms to weddings and funerals, can be seen as bridges punctuating major transitional phases and helping human beings to deal with the transience of their lives. For Freud, in disagreement with the pessimistic poet accompanying him on a walk, what he calls the "transience of all things" actually increases their beauty: "Limitation in the possibility of an enjoyment raises the value of the enjoyment," he wrote. "A flower that blossoms only for a single night does not seem to us on that account less lovely. Nor can I understand any better why the beauty and perfection of a work of art or of an intellectual achievement should lose its worth because of its temporal limitation" (Freud, 1916a, pp. 305–06).

I shall now briefly dwell on the relevance of the ideas outlined above in relation to some aspects of our psychoanalytic work. I will not even touch here, despite the fact that it is most relevant to our topic, on the notoriously thorny issue of how physiology and psychology relate to one another, as manifested in those phenomena located on the border between them, such as hypochondriacal and psychosomatic conditions, not to mention sexuality. All I will say is that the "mysterious leap" between body and mind, which by the way was also at the origins of the Freudian theory of conversion hysteria, has not been replaced yet, as far as I know, by any solid bridge.

Another controversial issue concerns the diagnosis of borderline personality disorder, a label given a variety of definitions by different clinicians. One that I find helpful suggests that borderline patients are those who operate as neurotics but use psychotic (i.e., more primitive) defence mechanisms, such as massive denial, splitting, and projective identification. One of my analysands, always in search of a label for her own condition, one day almost triumphantly announced to me: "At long last, I now think I know what I am: *a borderline!*" And after a minute of silent reflection she added in a sad tone of voice: "… the wrong side of it". I could not have found a better definition of her pathology.

Another relevant condition to be considered from our perspective is that of so-called manic flights, which I propose to compare here with Icarus's doomed attempts to fly too close to the sun.[1] Some individuals trapped in their own disproportionate narcissism get caught in a self-destructive upwards spiral of manic activity, flying higher and higher to avoid facing the panic of being unable to rejoin the object from which they have tried to separate and which thus becomes progressively unavailable. The further away such an object is, the more intense is the despair, the more urgent the need to use manic defences to avoid it. But these defensive activities are doomed to lead the subjects, not unlike the gamblers dangerously increasing their bets to cover their losses, even further away from the object with which they so desperately seek to reunite. The need of toddlers and adolescents to come back to their parents for "emotional refuelling", accurately observed by Margaret Mahler (Mahler, Pine & Bergman, 1975), refers to the children's exciting but also hazardous journeys of discovery of themselves and their surrounding world. However, when parents are unavailable, distant, or empty, such a refuelling becomes problematic. The way back to safety is eventually barred. The wax holding the wings of separation and individuation together gradually melts away in the heat of the sun, sometimes with catastrophic results.

In this light we could interpret manic activities not only as attempts to repair damaged objects, that is, to overcome guilt about aggressive attacks and therefore as defences from depressive anxiety, but also as attempts to recover lost objects—to deal with separation anxiety by trying to reunite the subjects with what they have lost. I would add that *manic* activities (and I include here quasi-normal sexual promiscuity in adolescents, frantic bursts of creativity in artists, and "workaholism" in psychoanalysts) are always also *magic* activities. Though at times they are not without a successful outcome, they are intrinsically unrealistic and the subject ends up further removed from its sources of nourishment and security. The drowning of Narcissus, of Icarus and of so many other young "rebels without a cause" might then be seen as the tragic manifestation of their unconscious need to return to the maternal womb.

A no less complex aspect of psychoanalytic work relevant to my musings concerns the transference. It can be seen as a meeting point, as a bridge across different temporalities: an instrument to interpret the present in order to reconstruct the past, as well as the manifestation of a past relived in the here-and-now of the analytic relationship. Transference is intrinsically associated to memory and to its centrality for our emotional life, inasmuch as memories take place in a transitional time between past and present, connecting them together.

A wonderful illustration of the importance of memories during and beyond our existence is provided by the Japanese film *Afterlife* (1998), directed by Hirokazu Kore-eda. As we learn from one of the opening scenes framing an emblematic square of pure light, the setting of the movie (on the surface a rather prosaic, dilapidated school) is in fact a metaphysical way-station between, or spatio-temporal bridge across, life and death. The guests of this institution, all people who have just died, are offered there a few days to select, with the help of responsible members of staff, one and just one meaningful memory from their individual past history, which a nearby studio will then turn into a video that the guests will eventually take away in their afterlife (Sabbadini & Stein, 2001).

A *trauma* occurs when the transition from one condition to the next, instead of taking place gradually—something that in musical terms would be described as a slow *crescendo* or *diminuendo*—is instead sudden and unexpected—*subito fortissimo*—for example, when we become victims of an accident, of a violent attack, or of an unpredicted natural catastrophe. In these cases it is as if the bridge that should have allowed a smooth and safe passage to the next stage has collapsed, and we were then left feeling as if the earth has opened up under our feet. In our clinical work it is our responsibility to provide a container for our analysands past and current traumatic experiences, but also to protect them from unnecessary exposure to mini-traumatic situations within the analysis itself. This we can do by offering them, for instance, a safe and consistent setting surrounded by rigorous (yet not rigid) boundaries, and by paying tactful attention to the timing of our interventions. Even the provision of a waiting room can in this respect be helpful in allowing our patients to experience a more gradual transition from the outside world to the analytic space.

I consider it important, if often also difficult, to interpret what happens in the *space* between the inside and the outside of my consulting room, and in the *time* between a session and what immediately precedes or follows it. Kate, the analysand of mine briefly discussed in Chapter One, never replied to my "hellos" when I met her in the waiting room nor to my "goodbyes" at the end of sessions. For her, doing so would have meant acknowledging the existence of an empty time between our meetings and of a gap between her and me; and, therefore, of the existence of a relationship between us. The breaks in Kate's experience of the analytic process—the transitional space/time between the waiting room and the consulting room, between the door and the couch and the door again, the spatio-temporal bridge between one session and the next—were magically denied.

As to what takes place inside our psychoanalytic rooms, we are familiar with those oscillatory movements, or crossings of the spatio-temporal bridges, when patients place themselves (and implicitly their listening analysts) in a discursive modality characterised by a tension between solipsistic monologue and interpersonal dialogue. Or between free associations and silence, the latter being another phenomenon well known to most of us. As described in Chapter Nine, I think of silence as a container of words, and believe that in analysis and everywhere else it can act as a weapon, a shield, or a bridge. What happens then between words? In the white spaces that separate them on the page, or the infinitesimally brief silences that separate them in the course of a conversation? And in music too, as we have seen in Chapter Ten, rests are as important as notes, providing meaningful links between them. What do we imagine is on a music score, between a note and a rest and the next note? Or what do we hear during a concert between the end of the vibrations of a note played on the violin and the beginning of the next one produced by the cello? While there would be no music if a pause became too long, without short intervals of silence there could be no music either.

* * *

Analogously, in the visual arts there could be no meaningful representation of form without shadows and so-called "negative spaces" around and in between shapes. And in written language there could be no meaningful representation of narrative without punctuation. Some of the work of graphic artists like M. C. Escher and of novelists like James Joyce or José Saramago can be considered as the exceptions that confirm the rule.

In movies too, if we exclude rare instances of unedited "real time" productions, the alternation of shots and sequences skilfully linked or separated through the process of editing has constituted the main visual form of storytelling throughout the first 120 years of the history of cinema. Let us remember here that cinema has emerged in the course of the nineteenth century through an organic development from the first hazy pictures of pioneer photographers such as Louis Daguerre, Fox Talbot, and George Eastman, to the sequences of photographic images by experimental artists Eadweard Muybridge and Étienne-Jules Marey, to the films of the Lumière brothers (the first screenings of which, in 1895, made the birth of cinema chronologically coincide with that of psychoanalysis itself). Since then, cinema has undergone, and is still undergoing, a process of multiple transformations, with transitional periods between its different stages, and bridges linking them together: from silent to talkies, from black-and-white to colour, from analogue to digital, from 35 millimeter celluloid to video and then DVD, from 2D through HD to 3D ....

While cinema was born at the end of the nineteenth century, the *idea* of cinema goes back more than two millennia, when Plato (c.360 BC) used the "Simile of the Cave" to describe how chained prisoners, unable to move or turn their heads backwards, would mistakenly believe that the wooden and stone statues carried in front of a fire placed behind them, and whose shadows were thus projected on the cave wall facing them, were real people and not simulacra. "And so in every way", Plato concluded, "they would believe that the shadows of the objects we mentioned were the whole truth" (Plato, c.360 BC, p. 241). Jean-Louis Baudry (1970), a prominent Lacanian film scholar, also refers to Plato's myth in developing his own views about what he calls the cinema "apparatus"—a concept I could relate to that of the spatio-temporal bridge in so far as it constitutes a necessary, creative link between the filmmakers' imagination and their filmic products, and between the latter and their audience. Baudry's influential apparatus theory emphasised the ideological nature of the mechanics of film representation. In particular the camera and the editing suite were considered by Baudry and his followers to be key tools in providing ideological points of view to the spectators' gaze, thus making cinema itself an instrumental bridge for the transmission of dominant cultural values.

What spreads out in front of the cinematographer's eyes and separates her from the scene she is in the process of shooting—but, at the same time, also keeps her in contact with it—is another instance of spatio-temporal bridges. A territory that will soon no longer be occupied by the images framed by the camera, but which is not yet occupied by the final product to be eventually projected on the screen. Similarly, for the audience collectively immersed in the regressive darkness of the movie theatre this space and time of play and creativity is to be found, following the beam of light that originates in the projection room, between their gaze and the silver screen. Sitting in the cinema armchair, and at the same time placing their minds and hearts inside the film story, the spectators find themselves occupying a productively ambiguous mental space. Furthermore, our metaphorical bridge connects not only the world of external reality with its filmed representation, but also the latter with the reality perceived by the viewers' gaze—a reality, by the way, which is illusory in more than one sense of the word. Contrary to our impression movies don't move at all, for they are composed of sequences of twenty-four still frames per second, separated by imperceptibly small gaps. Lights and shadows flicker in the cinema theatre, this no-man's land between spectator and spectacle; this territory as mysterious, fascinating (and also a little frightening) as the setting of the primal scene; a spatio-temporal bridge where films can contain our anxieties, nourish our minds, and even transform our lives (Sabbadini, 2011).

It may be relevant to observe here that there is a similarity between the film screen and what Bertram D. Lewin (1953) described as a *dream screen*, in that they are places of both fusion and separation (Eberwein, 1984). Besides, movies and dreams seem to share a morphological equivalence in so far as both can be considered to express latent unconscious wishes through their manifest contents, and both use, for the purpose of circumventing repression, similar mechanisms. These include (in films, especially at the editing stage) condensation, displacement, symbolic representation, secondary revision, and distortions of time and space. Condensation is particularly relevant here in so far as one of its functions (in dreams as elsewhere, such as in symptom-formation) is to launch a bridge between two thoughts, words, or people by creating a composite one with features belonging to both. "The construction of collective and composite figures is one of the chief methods by which condensation operates in dreams", writes Freud (1900, p. 293). And again: "An *intermediate common entity* had been constructed which admitted of multiple determination" (Freud, 1900a, p. 295; my emphasis).

*  *  *

While it would be arrogant to claim that psychoanalysis has privileged access to a critical interpretation of any given creative product, it might prove useful to link the relative universality of the human thirst for knowledge to that of the Oedipus constellation. In this respect we could suggest that we create, with varying degrees of success, not only in order to repair damage to internal objects (as some Kleinian thinkers have suggested) but also to help ourselves resolve the insoluble dilemmas inherent in the oedipal complex: to impress one of our parents, punish the other, compete with or reward them both and, more specifically, recover the lost objects of our primary loves and identifications. To succeed, in other words, where Icarus had failed.

Artists, furthermore, often have a real or imaginary partner (a muse, or the audience in their minds) whose presence indicates the triangular, and therefore oedipal, nature of their activity. Babies, literary or otherwise, are always conceived by two parents. It should not be difficult to recognise the only thinly disguised oedipal significance of the content of much artistic production, from Greek tragedy and Renaissance paintings to Romantic novels, Italian operas and Hollywood movies. This third party, if we allow ourselves to shift to a different metaphor, may not necessarily be found in the primal scene bedroom, but in the Socratic labour room. The artist would need the sympathetic presence of a midwife providing the necessary conditions, amidst some una- voidable labour pains, for the baby to be delivered. In this function, she would be similar to psychoanalysts offering their analysands a safe therapeutic setting—or indeed to any parents facilitating for their chil- dren the exploration of a transitional space and time where and when real playing is possible. In this respect I think Winnicott's ideas can be further extended by suggesting that the space and time of play are not just those placed between individuals and their environment, but also those located among different aspects of the self (the emotional, the physical, and the intellectual) that would thus find a new if precarious balance in each work of art.

In this search for equilibrium we can come across a common mani- festation of narcissism, known as perfectionism. While in moderate dosage (perfectionism in its imperfect form, as it were) it could facilitate creativity, as soon as it takes on a more obsessional quality it becomes an obstacle to it. Many potentially creative people never produce any- thing because they are too concerned that it would not live up to their own unrealistic standards. For them, to be good enough is just not good enough.

When discussing creativity from a psychoanalytic perspective, some- times we forget the creative aspects of our psychoanalytic work itself. In the consistent, and therefore relatively safe, time and space provided by our "studios", our main analytic functions include attentive listening, thinking in a state of relaxed concentration, reflecting on the emotional reactions that words and silences evoke in us and our patients, and, occasionally, talking. Our task involves the creative use of the material brought to us by our patients, in combination with that brought to ses- sions by our own personal and professional experience. We make links among different aspects of their lives—from different periods in their histories and belonging to different areas in their minds. Through the use of transference interpretations we make sense of the remembered childhood in terms of the present, and of the here-and-now of the thera- peutic relationship in relation to the past. Much psychoanalytic narra- tive centres around the same themes as much literature and drama (and films, and operas): love and death, conflicts of loyalties, travelling as a metaphor for life, an ambivalent relationship with our bodies and those of others, the pain of being torn between desires and a sense of duty. In our analytic work we are editors involved in the selection, cutting and pasting together of dissociated fragments, out of which we help recreate old pictures—or create new ones. We build relationships with people whose main problem is an incapacity to keep them going—and we make them the focus of our understanding. As if we were musicians, we help our analysands to enrich with sounds the frightening silence of the void they carry inside. Like painters, we bring some colour to the greyness of their depression. Not unlike archaeologists, or biographers, we excavate in order to reconstruct. We try to make rational sense of what feels incomprehensible and mad. We tolerate within ourselves the anxiety of not knowing, and with our example we help others to stay with unresolved uncertainties without manically rushing to self-destructive enactments. When we can, we translate the obscure idiom of psychological symptoms and somatisations, of dreams and parapraxes, into a more comprehensible language, in an attempt to integrate disintegrated regions of our analysands' internal worlds.

The empty canvas before it gets flooded with colour.

The quiet concert hall as the conductor lifts the baton in the air at the beginning of a concert.

The blank page, or computer screen, before words start leaving their marks on it.

# NOTES

## Introduction

1. For instance, Freud's paper on technique *Zur Einleitung der Behandlung* (1913c) is translated as *On beginning the treatment*. The noun "treatment(s)" and the verb "to treat" can be found over 1,800 times in the *Standard Edition*.
2. While I object to the term "treatment" in psychoanalytic language, I use without too many problems (though perhaps a little inconsistently) other words such as "therapy" or "patient". I do not understand these in connection with their medical meaning, only attributed to them in more recent times, but rather keeping in mind their original etymology: "therapy" derives from the Greek verb *therapeuo* which means "to care for, to be concerned about", and "patient" from the noun *pathos* which describes "experience, passion or suffering".
3. See Freud, S., *The question of lay analysis* (1926e).
4. *The Concise Oxford Dictionary, 7th Edition* (1964): Oxford: Oxford University Press, 1982.

## Chapter One

1. See also Chapter Eleven.
2. This and all other names of patients throughout this book have been changed. Other biographical details may also have been altered in order to protect the patients' anonymity.

## Chapter Two

1. There is a superb literary description of it in Salman Rushdie's novel *Midnight's Children* (1981).
2. In Chapter Ten I will suggest that the formation of a sense of identity in the baby depends not only on this process of visual *mirroring* of the mother's face, but also on a parallel process of auditory *echoing* of her voice.
3. Cain and Cain offer a different interpretation of this age factor, important in all instances of replacement children, when they state that "the death of an infant makes less likely some of the later comparisons, identification, etc., than would be the case where fully developed, older children, with distinctive traits, features, and achievements have died" (Cain and Cain, 1964, p. 455).
4. In a sense, writing this chapter was my attempt to satisfy my own curiosity and to deal with my own (as well as Renate's) anxieties about being left in the dark over such a crucial aspect of her life, and its effects on her personality and psychopathology, by focusing my intellectual and emotional attention upon it, by formulating relevant questions to myself, and by suggesting some provisional answers.
5. Both are of course also present in the Greek myth of Narcissus and in one of its modern counterparts, Oscar Wilde's novel *The Picture of Dorian Gray* (1890).
6. In Poe's story, the main character meets in his childhood a double who follows him around and persecutes him throughout his life. Eventually, at a masked ball, Wilson in exasperation plunges his sword into his double's breast, only to hear him say: "*In me didst thou exist; and, in my death, see by this image, which is thine own, how utterly thou hast murdered thyself*" (Poe, 1839, p. 178).

   In Dostoyevsky's novel (*The Double*), its protagonist Golyadkin develops a paranoid relationship with a character identical to himself, but who seems to always succeed instead of him. He becomes increasingly confused and persecuted by his own projections, until he ends up hallucinating "an endless string of Golyadkins all exactly alike" (Dostoyevsky, 1846, p. 284).

In Conrad's story, the double whom the Captain rescues from the sea and hides in his cabin is the embodiment not so much of an accusing conscience, but of a more instinctive and primitive unconscious side of his personality: "It was, in the night, as though I had been faced by my own reflection in the depths of a somber and immense mirror" (Conrad, 1910, p. 27).

In Schnitzler's novel the aged Venetian playboy can for a moment delude himself to be still the legendary Casanova of his *Mémoires* through identification with his younger double Lorenzi. Schnitzler (1862–1931) is of particular interest to us because he was a Viennese physician contemporary of Freud. Apparently the two felt a mixture of attraction and diffidence for each other. "I think I have avoided you from a kind of reluctance to meet my double," confessed Freud in a letter to him (Freud, 1922, in E. Freud, Ed. 1961, p. 344). For more about the relationship between Freud and Schnitzler, see Beharriell (1962).

Space only allows me to mention here the names of authors such as E. T. A. Hoffman, Robert L. Stevenson, Luigi Pirandello, Jorge L. Borges and Italo Calvino, so many of whose characters are confronted by their doubles in situations ranging from the grotesque to the tragic. A collection of good short stories on the theme of the double is the one edited by Richardson (1987).

7. Among theatre classics, we should mention Plautus (*Menaechmi*, c.206 BC), Shakespeare (*Comedy of Errors*, c.1592) and Goldoni (*I due gemelli veneziani*, 1747). Two cinematic masterpieces in this genre are Alfred Hitchcock's psychological thriller *The Wrong Man* (1956) and the impressive war epic by Akiri Kurosawa, *Kagamusha* (1980).

8. In comparing them to neurotics, Freud states that primitive people "regard a name as an essential part of a man's personality and as an important possession ... They are afraid of the presence or of the return of the dead person's ghost; and they ... feel that to utter his name is equivalent to invoking him and will quickly be followed by his presence. And accordingly they do everything they can to avoid any such evocation" (Freud, 1912c, pp. 56–57).

## Chapter Three

1. It seems ironic, in this respect, that throughout the history of Western art the image of the Virgin should be associated with the presence of her Child.

2. On a humorous note, I am reminded here of the joke about the boy chatting up a girl he has just met in a pub. As he introduces himself to

her as a student, an Arsenal supporter, and a non-practising Jew, she replies that she is an actress, a vegetarian, and a non-practising virgin.
3. See for instance, in this respect, the frightening French folktale of Bluebeard's castle.

## Chapter Six

1. This calendar is based on the assumption that the birthday of Jesus Christ took place in the year conventionally called 1AD. This assumption, though, is now being disputed: modern scholars, such as J. Fleming of The Hebrew University of Jerusalem, believe that Christ may have been born twelve years earlier. His evidence includes "a reference in the Book of Matthew that says King Herod was alive at the time; he is believed to have died in 4BC. In addition the census that the Book of Luke said brought Mary and Joseph to Bethlehem probably was carried out in the year 12 BC ... Halley's comet was visible in the year 10 BC when scholars suggest Christ would have been about two years old" *(The Guardian*, 21 December 1985).
2. The Crisis Centre run in North London by the Arbours Association.
3. Such issues are not simply political or technological, but philosophical. Phipps believes that "when we say 'time is running out', we are in fact referring to a specific notion of time, a peculiarly Western temporal norm" (Phipps, 1986, p. 122). This norm, which I have referred to previously, is based upon a view of time as having an irreversible direction, as beginning with Genesis and ending in the eschatological perspective of the Apocalypse. Cyclical time, instead, predominant in most pre-Christian and non-Christian cultures, is closer to timelessness and could contain no doomsday. "The imminent nuclear apocalypse, translated into time language, signifies a change in temporal outlook ... Just as the prophets of doom 2,000 years ago mistook a temporal change [from cyclical to linear time] for a literal apocalyptic end of the world (seen in terms of an Act of God), so the nuclear prophets of doom tend to interpret the end in literal, positivist terms (as an act of man). Nothing is more unsettling or disturbing than a change in temporal outlook; it feels like the end of all time" (Phipps, 1986, p. 123). In other words, "the Bomb is a time bomb" (Phipps, 1986, p. 125).

## Chapter Seven

1. According to the so-called Wolf Man, Freud had at first devised a different setting for his sessions: "Freud told me that he had originally sat

at the opposite end of the couch, so that analyst and analysand could look at each other. One female patient, exploiting this situation, made all possible—or rather impossible—attempts to seduce him. To rule out anything similar, once and for all, Freud moved from his earlier position to the opposite end of the couch" (Wolf-Man, 1971, p. 142). The authenticity of this account though, seems doubtful: not only because it comes from a not very reliable source, but also because it has not been confirmed by anyone else and is anyway inconsistent with the main functions of the couch.

2. See the rich literature on this subject reviewed by Stern (1978).

3. I have found in the literature disparate views about the link between forms of psychopathology and use of the couch. For instance, Saul (1958) warns against recommending it to schizoid personalities; Caligor and Wittenberg (1967) are against using it with obsessive-compulsive patients; Boyer (1966) reports treating many psychotics on the couch and Chessick (1971) describes his work with fourteen borderline patients in the reclining position. Spotniz (1969) believes that the personality of the therapist is in this respect a more important variable than the pathology of the patient.

4. According to Bion, everyone on the couch is afraid of assaults from the analyst, not just verbal or symbolic but physical ones too (Elizabeth Spillius, personal communication, 1984).

## Chapter Eight

1. It is methodologically correct, I believe, to make inferences about normal experience from pathology, in so far as there is a *continuum* between the two: indeed, most psychoanalytic theories of normality are based upon clinical observations of psychopathology.

2. Following Freud's reformulation of his drive theory (1920g), one might attempt to demonstrate a link between castration anxiety and life drives on the one hand, and what I termed possession anxiety and the death drive on the other. Libidinal drives, functioning according to the pleasure/unpleasure principle, would then be associated with the anxiety of losing the object or its love, cathected with libido; whereas the death drive would colour the object (the other person, the self, or one's identity, body or genitals) with negative, destructive and frightening connotations, and turn its very possession into a source of anxiety.

3. A similar argument could of course be applied to other pairs of opposites too, such as exhibitionism and scopophilia.

## Chapter Ten

1. A number of articles are scattered through scientific journals, such as the *Psychoanalytic Quarterly* and the *International Review of Psycho-Analysis*. A good selection on the subject can be found in the two volumes on *Psychoanalytic Explorations in Music* edited by Feder, Karmel and Pollock (1990; 1993).

## Chapter Eleven

1. According to the well-known Greek legend, Icarus dares to fly away from his father, the inventor Daedalus, with wings held together by wax. Like many other adolescents, he refuses to listen to Daedalus' advice not to do so: the wax will melt if he flies too low and close to the waves of the sea, or too high and close to the heat of the sun—places equivalent to the "low" depressive and "high" manic conditions, respectively. Icarus's disobedience costs him his life.

# REFERENCES

Abraham, G. (1976). The sense and concept of time in psychoanalysis. *International Review of Psycho-Analysis, 3*: 461–472.

Abraham, K. (1919). A particular form of neurotic resistance against the psycho-analytic method. In: *Selected Papers on Psycho-analysis* (pp. 303–311). London: Hogarth, 1949.

Abraham, K. (1922). Manifestations of the female castration complex. *The International Journal of Psychoanalysis, 3*: 1–29.

Abrams, D. (1993). Freud and Max Graf: On the psychoanalysis of music. In: S. Feder, R. Karmel, & G. Pollock (Eds.) *Psychoanalytic Explorations in Music: Second Series*. New York: International Universities Press.

Alighieri, D. (1300). *La Divina Commedia, Vol. 1: Inferno*. Firenze: La Nuova Italia, 1965.

Antinucci-Mark, G. (1986). Some thoughts on the similarities between psychotherapy and theatre scenarios. *British Journal of Psychotherapy, 3*: 14–19.

Anzieu, D. (1985). *Le Moi-peau*. Paris: Dunod; Engl. transl. *The Skin Ego*. New Haven, CT: Yale University Press, 1989.

Arlow, J. A. (1961). Silence and the theory of technique. *Journal of the American Psychoanalytic Association, 9*: 44–55.

Arlow, J. A. (1984). Disturbances of the sense of time, with special reference to the experience of timelessness. *Psychoanalytic Quarterly, 53*: 13–37.

Arlow, J. A. (1986). Psychoanalysis and time. *Journal of the American Psychoanalytic Association, 34*: 507–528.

Aruffo, R. N. (1995). The couch: Reflections from an interactional view of analysis. *Psychoanalytic Inquiry, 15*: 369–385.

Balint, M. (1968). *The Basic Fault: Therapeutic Aspects of Regression*. London: Tavistock, 1979.

Baudry, J. L. (1970). Ideological effects of the basic cinematographic apparatus. *Film Quarterly, 28* (2) (Winter, 1974–1975), pp. 39–47.

Beharriell, F. (1962). Freud's 'double': Arthur Schnitzler. *Journal of the American Psychoanalytic Association, 10*: 722–730.

Berenstein, I. (1987). Analysis terminable and interminable, fifty years on. *The International Journal of Psycho-Analysis, 68*: 21–35.

Bernau, A. (2007a). *Virgins: A Cultural History*. London: Granta.

Bernau, A. (2007b). Eternally virginal. *The Guardian*, Wednesday 18 July.

Bettelheim, B. (1976). *The Uses of Enchantment: The Meaning and Importance of Fairy Tales*. Harmondsworth: Penguin.

Birksted-Breen, D. (1996). Phallus, penis and mental space. *The International Journal of Psychoanalysis, 77*: 649–657.

Birksted-Breen, D. (2003). Time and the après-coup. *The International Journal of Psychoanalysis, 84*: 1501–1515.

Bloch, M. (1939). *La Société Féodale: La Formation des Liens de Dépendance*. Paris: A. Michel.

Blos, P. (1972). Silence: A clinical exploration. *The Psychoanalytic Quarterly, 41*: 348–363.

Bonovitz, C. (2007). Termination never ends: The inevitable incompleteness of psychoanalysis. *Contemporary Psychoanalysis, 43*: 229–246.

Bowlby, J. (1969). *Attachment and Loss. Volume 1: Attachment*. Harmondsworth: Pelican.

Boyer, L. B. (1966). Office treatment of schizophrenic patients by psychoanalysis. *The Psychoanalytic Forum, 1*: 337–346.

Cain, A., & Cain, B. (1964). On replacing a child. *Journal of the American Academy of Child and Adolescent Psychiatry, 3*: 443–456.

Caligor, L., & Wittenberg, E. (1967). The interpersonal approach with particular emphasis on the obsessional. In: B. Wolman (Ed.) *Psychoanalytic Techniques*. New York: Basic Books.

Carels, N. (2009). Du silence en psychanalyse vers la psychanalyse du silence. *Revue Belge de Psychanalyse, 54*: 17–29.

Carlino, R. (2011). *Distance Psychoanalysis*. London: Karnac.

Carroll, L. (1865). *Alice's Adventures in Wonderland*. London: Macmillan.

Cavafy, C. P. (1911). Ithaka. In: G. Savidis (Ed.) *Collected Poems* [Translated by E. Keeley & P. Sherrard]. Princeton, NJ: Princeton University Press, 1992.

Celenza, A. (2005). Vis-à-vis the couch: Where is psychoanalysis? *The International Journal of Psychoanalysis, 86*: 1645–1659.

Cheshire, N. M. (1996). The empire of the ear: Freud's problem with music. *The International Journal of Psychoanalysis, 77*: 1127–1168.

Chessick, R. D. (1971). Use of the couch in the psychotherapy of borderline patients. *Archives of General Psychiatry, 25*: 307–313.

Cohn, N. (1970). *The Pursuit of the Millennium: Revolutionary Millenarians and Mystical Anarchists of the Middle Ages.* London: Paladin.

Colarusso, C. A. (1987). The development of time sense: From object constancy to adolescence. *Journal of the American Psychoanalytic Association, 35*: 119–144.

Conrad, J. (1910). *Heart of Darkness* and *The Secret Sharer*. New York: Signet.

Cremerius, J. (1969). Schweigen als probleme der psychoanalytischen technik. *Jahrbuch der Psychoanalyse, 6*: 69–103.

Dalí, S., & Parinaud, A. (1973). *The Unspeakable Confessions of Salvador Dalí.* London: Allen, 1976.

De Simone, G. (1994). *Ending Analysis: Theory and Technique.* London: Karnac, 1997.

Deutsch, H. (1944–45). *The Psychology of Women: A Psychoanalytic Interpretation, Vols. 1 & 2.* New York: Grune & Stratton.

Diaz de Chumaceiro, C. (1992). On Freud's admiration for Beethoven and his 'splendid creations'. *American Journal of Psychoanalysis, 52*: 175–181.

Diaz de Chumaceiro (1993). Richard Wagner's life and music: What Freud knew. In: S. Feder, R. L. Karmel, & G. H. Pollock (Eds.) *Psychoanalytical Explorations in Music* (Second Series) (pp. 249–278). New York: International Universities Press.

Dostoyevsky, F. (1846). *The Double.* Harmondsworth: Penguin, 1972.

Duby, G. (1967). *L'An Mil.* Paris: Julliard.

Eberwein, R. T. (1984). *Film and The Dream Screen: A Sleep and a Forgetting.* Princeton: Princeton University Press.

Eliot, T. S. (1944). Burnt Norton. In: *Four Quartets* (pp. 11–18). London: Faber, 1959.

Feder, S., Karmel, R. L., & Pollock, G. H. (Eds.) (1990). *Psychoanalytical Explorations in Music.* New York: International Universities Press.

Feder, S., Karmel, R. L., & Pollock, G. H. (Eds.) (1993). *Psychoanalytical Explorations in Music* (Second Series). New York: International Universities Press.

Ferenczi, S. (1911). On obscene words. In: *First Contributions to Psychoanalysis* (pp. 132–153). London: Maresfield Reprints, 1980.

Ferenczi, S. (1916–17). Silence is golden. In: *Further Contributions to the Theory and Technique of Psycho-analysis* (pp. 250–251). London: Maresfield Reprints, 1980.

Ferraro, F., & Garella, A. (2001). *In-fine: Saggio sulla conclusione dell'analisi*. Rome: Franco Angeli.

Festinger, L., Riecken, H. W., & Schatter, S. (1956). *When Prophecy Fails*. New York: Harper & Row, 1964.

Fliess, R. (1949). Silence and verbalization: A supplement to the theory of the analytic rule. *The International Journal of Psychoanalysis, 30*: 21–30.

Focillon, H. (1952). *L'An Mil*. Paris: Armand Colin.

Frank, A. (1995). The couch, psychoanalytic process, and psychic change: A case study. *Psychoanalytic Inquiry, 15*: 324–337.

Freud, E. (Ed.) (1961). *Letters of Sigmund Freud, 1873–1939*. London: Hogarth.

Freud, M. (1957). *Glory Reflected: Sigmund Freud, Man and Father*. London: Angus & Robertson.

Freud, S. (1893b). The psychotherapy of hysteria. *S. E., 2*: (253–305). London: Hogarth.

Freud, S. (1900a). *The Interpretation of Dreams (First Part)*. *S. E., 4*. London: Hogarth.

Freud, S. (1901b). *The Psychopathology of Everyday Life*. *S. E., 6*. London: Hogarth.

Freud, S. (1909b). Analysis of a phobia in a five-year-old boy. *S. E., 10*: 5–149. London: Hogarth.

Freud, S. (1911c). Psycho-analytic notes on an autobiographical account of a case of paranoia (dementia paranoides). *S. E., 12*: 3–82. London: Hogarth.

Freud, S. (1912c). *Totem and Taboo*. *S. E., 13*: 1–162. London: Hogarth.

Freud, S. (1913c). On beginning the treatment. *S. E., 12*: 123–141. London: Hogarth.

Freud, S. (1914b). The Moses of Michelangelo. *S. E., 13*: 209–238. London: Hogarth.

Freud, S. (1915b). Thoughts for the times on war and death. *S. E., 14*: 273–302. London: Hogarth Press.

Freud, S. (1915e). The unconscious. *S. E., 14*: 159–204. London: Hogarth.

Freud, S. (1916a). On transience. *S. E., 14*: 305–307. London: Hogarth.

Freud, S. (1916d). Some character-types met with in psycho-analytic work. *S. E., 14*: 309–333. London: Hogarth.

Freud, S. (1917e). Mourning and Melancholia. *S. E., 14*: 237–258. London: Hogarth.

Freud, S. (1918a). The taboo of virginity. *S. E., 11*: 191–208. London: Hogarth.

Freud, S. (1919h). The 'Uncanny'. *S. E., 17*: 217–256. London: Hogarth.

Freud, S. (1920g). Beyond the pleasure principle. *S. E., 18*: 1–64. London: Hogarth.

Freud, S. (1924d). The dissolution of the Oedipus complex. *S. E., 19*: 171–179. London: Hogarth.

Freud, S. (1926d). Inhibitions, symptoms and anxiety. *S. E., 20*: 75–172. London: Hogarth.

Freud, S. (1926e). The question of lay analysis. *S. E., 20*: 177–250. London: Hogarth.

Freud, S. (1927e). Fetishism. *S. E., 21*: 149–155. London: Hogarth.

Freud, S. (1928b). Dostoevsky and parricide. *S. E., 21*: 175–198. London: Hogarth.

Freud, S. (1930a). Civilization and its discontents. *S. E., 21*: 57–146. London: Hogarth.

Freud, S. (1933a). *New Introductory Lectures on Psycho-analysis. S. E., 22.* London: Hogarth.

Freud, S. (1936a). A disturbance of memory on the Acropolis. *S. E., 22*: 239–248. London: Hogarth.

Freud, S. (1937c). Analysis terminable and interminable. *S. E., 23*: 209–253. London: Hogarth.

Freud S., & Breuer, J. (1895d). *Studies on Hysteria. S. E., 2.* London: Hogarth.

Gabbard, G. O. (2009). What is a "good enough" termination? *Journal of the American Psychoanalytic Association, 57*: 575–594.

Gay, P. (1988). *Freud: A Life for Our Time.* London: Macmillan.

Gifford, S. (1960). Sleep, time and the early ego: Comments on the development of the 24-hour sleep-wakefulness pattern as a precursor of ego functioning. *Journal of the American Psychoanalytic Association, 8*: 5–42.

Gilbert, M. (1987). *The Holocaust.* Glasgow: Fontana/Collins.

Glocer Fiorini, L., & Canestri, J. (Eds.) (2009). *The Experience of Time: Psycho-analytic Perspectives.* London: Karnac.

Graf, M. (1957). *Jede Stunde War Erfüllt: Ein halbes Jahrhundert Musik-und Theaterleben.* Wien-Frankfurt: Forum-Verlag.

Green, A. (1979). Le silence du psychanalyste. *Topique, 23*: 5–25.

Green, A. (2000). *Le Temps Éclaté.* Paris: Éditions de Minuit.

Greenson, R. R. (1961). On the silence and sounds of the analytic hour. *Journal of the American Psychoanalytic Association, 9*: 79–84.

Greenson, R. R. (1967). *The Technique and Practice of Psychoanalysis.* London: Hogarth.

Grotstein, J. S. (1995). A reassessment of the couch in psychoanalysis. *Psychoanalytic Inquiry, 15*: 396–405.

Gruen, A. (1967). The couch or the man. *Psychoanalytic Review, 54*: 72–79.

H. D. (1956). *Tribute to Freud*. Manchester: Carcanet, 1985.

Hall, R., & Closson, W. (1964). An experimental study of the couch. *Journal of Nervous and Mental Disease, 138*: 474–480.

Hárnik, J. (1925). Die triebhaft-affektiven Momente in Zeitgefühl. *Imago, 11*: 32–57.

Hartocollis, P. (1972) Time as a dimention of affects. *Journal of the American Psychoanalytic Association, 20*: 92–108.

Hartocollis, P. (1974). Origins of time: A reconstruction of the ontogenetic development of the sense of time based on object-relations theory. *Psychoanalytic Quarterly, 43*: 243–261.

Hartocollis, P. (1975). Time and affect in psychopathology. *Journal of the American Psychoanalytic Association, 23*: 383–395.

Hartocollis, P. (1983). *Time and Timelessness or the Varieties of Temporal Experience*. New York: International Universities Press.

Holtzman, D., & Kulish, N. (1996). Nevermore: The hymen and the loss of virginity. *Journal of the American Psychoanalytic Association, 44*: 303–332.

Horney, K. (1933). The denial of the vagina. *The International Journal of Psychoanalysis, 14*: 57–70.

Humphrey, N., & Lifton, R. J. (Eds.) (1984). *In a Dark Time*. London/Boston: Faber.

Illich, I. (1975). *Medical Nemesis: The Expropriation of Health*. London: Calder & Boyars.

Innes-Smith, J. (1987). Time and terminability in the psychoanalytic process. [Unpublished paper].

Jacobson, E. (1964). *The Self and the Object World*. Madison, CT: International Universities Press.

Jones, E. (1953). *Sigmund Freud: Life and Work, Vol. 1*. London: Hogarth, 1980.

Jones, E. (1957). *Sigmund Freud. Life and Work, Vol. 3*. London: Hogarth, 1980.

Jung, C. G. (1961). *Memories, Dreams, Reflections*. London: Fontana, 1967.

Kelman, H. (1954). The use of the analytic couch. *American Journal of Psychoanalysis, 14*: 65–82.

Khan, M. R. (1963). Silence as communication. In: *The Privacy of the Self* (pp. 168–180). London: Hogarth, 1974.

Klein, M. (1923). Early analysis. In: *The Writings of Melanie Klein, Vol. 1* (pp. 76–105). London: Hogarth.

Kris, E. (1952). *Psychoanalytic Explorations in Art*. New York: International Universities Press.

Kundera, M. (1984). *The Unbearable Lightness of Being*. [Translated by M. H. Heim]. London: Faber, 1985.

Lable, I. Kelley, J. M., Ackerman, J., Levy, R., Waldron, S., & Ablon, J. S. (2010). The role of the couch in psychoanalysis: Proposed research designs and some preliminary data. *Journal of the American Psychoanalytic Association, 58*: 861–887.

Lacan, J. (1949). The mirror stage as formative of the function of the I as revealed in psychoanalytic experience. In: A Sheridan (Trans) *Écrits: A Selection*. New York: Norton, 1977.

Laget, A. (1995). *Freud et le Temps*. Lyon: Presses Universitaires de Lyon.

Laing, R. D. (1967). *The Politics of Experience* and *The Bird of Paradise*. Harmondsworth: Penguin.

Langer, S. K. (1957). *Problems of Art*. New York: Scribner.

Langs, R. (1973). *The Technique of Psychoanalytic Psychotherapy*. New York: Aronson.

Leira, T. (1995). Silence and communication: nonverbal dialogue and therapeutic action. *The Scandinavian Psychoanalytic Review, 18*: 41–65.

Lemma, A., & Caparrotta, L. (Eds.) (2013). *Psychoanalysis in the Technoculture Era*. Hove: Routledge.

Levy, K. (1958). Silence in the analytic session. *The International Journal of Psychoanalysis, 39*: 50–58.

Lewin, B. D. (1953). Reconsideration of the dream screen. *Psychoanalytic Quarterly, 22*: 174–199.

Liberman, D. (1955). Acerca de la percepción del tiempo. *Revista Psico-analítica, 12*: 370–375.

Lingiardi, V., & Bei, F. D. (2011). Questioning the couch: Historical and clinical perspectives. *Psychoanalytic Psychology, 28*: 389–404.

Mahler, M., Pine, F., & Bergman, A. (1975). *The Psychological Birth of the Human Infant*. London: Hutchinson.

McCann, L. (1984). *Nostradamus: The Man who Saw Through Time*. London: Panther.

McDonald, M. (1970). Transitional tunes and musical development. *The Psychoanalytic Study of the Child, 25*: 503–520. (Also in Feder *et al.*, 1990).

McDougall, J. (1982). *Théâtre du Je*. Paris: Gallimard.

Mintz, I. (1971). The anniversary reaction: A response to the unconscious sense of time. *Journal of the American Psychoanalytic Association, 19*: 720–735.

Mojtabai, A. G. (1986). *Blessed Assurance: At Home With the Bomb in Amarillo, Texas*. Boston: Houghton Mifflin.

Nagera, H. (1967). *Vincent van Gogh: A Psychological Study*. London: George, Allen & Unwin.

Nagera, H. (1969). The imaginary companion: Its significance for ego development and conflict solution. *The Psychoanalytic Study of the Child, 24*: 165–196.

Namnum, A. (1972). Time in psychoanalytic technique. *Journal of the American Psychoanalytic Association, 20*: 736–750.

Nasio, J. D. (Ed.) (1987). *Le Silence en Psychanalyse.* Paris: Rivages.

Nass, M. (1984). The development of creative imagination in composers. *International Review of Psycho-Analysis, 11*: 481–492. (Also in Feder *et al.*, 1990).

Noy, P. (1968). The development of musical ability. *The Psychoanalytical Study of the Child, 23*: 332–347. (Also in Feder *et al.*, 1990).

Oremland, J. D. (1975). An unexpected result of the analysis of a talented musician. *The Psychoanalytic Study of the Child, 30*: 375–407.

Orgel, S. (2000). Letting go: Some thoughts about termination. *Journal of the American Psychoanalytic Association, 48*: 719–738.

Orwell, G. (1949). *Nineteen Eighty-Four.* Harmondsworth: Penguin, 1954.

Perelberg, R. J. (2008). *Time, Space and Phantasy.* Hove: Routledge.

Phillips, D. P., & Feldman, K. A. (1973). A dip in deaths before ceremonial occasions: Some new relationships between social integration and mortality. *American Sociological Review, 38*: 678–696.

Phipps, J. F. (1986). Time and the bomb. In: I. Fenton (Ed.) *The Psychology of Nuclear Conflict* (pp. 118–131). London: Coventure.

Piontelli, A. (1992). *From Fetus to Child: An Observational and Psychoanalytic Study.* London: Routledge.

Plato (c. 360 B.C.). *The Republic* [Translated and introduced by Desmond Lee] (Part 7, Para 7, pp. 240–248). Harmondsworth: Penguin, 1955.

Poe, E. A. (1839). William Wilson. In: D. Galloway (Ed.) *Selected Writings of Edgar Allan Poe* (pp. 158–178). Harmondsworth: Penguin, 1967.

Poe, E. A. (1845). The purloined letter. In: D. Galloway (Ed.) *Selected Writings of Edgar Allan Poe* (pp. 330–349). Harmondsworth: Penguin, 1967.

Prensky, M. (2001). Digital natives, digital immigrants (Part 1). *On the Horizon, 9*: 1–6.

Rank, O. (1925). *The Double: A Psychoanalytic Study.* Chapel Hill, NC: The University of North Carolina Press, 1971.

Reale, P. (1984). *Ricerche Sperimentali sulla Nozione di Tempo.* Bologna: Pàtron Editore.

Reik, T. (1926). In the beginning is silence. In: *The Inner Experience of a Psychoanalyst.* London: George Allen & Unwin, 1949.

Reik, T. (1948). *Listening with the Third Ear: The Inner Experience of a Psychoanalyst.* New York: Grove.

Reik, T. (1953). *The Haunting Melody: Psychoanalytic Experiences in Life and Music.* New York: Farrar, Straus & Young.

Richardson, M. (1987). *Double/Double.* Harmondsworth: Penguin.

Robertiello, R. (1967). The couch. *Psychoanalytic Review, 54*: 69–71.

Ronningstam, E. (2006). Silence. *The International Journal of Psychoanalysis, 87*: 1277–1295.

Rose, G. J. (1992). *The Power of Form: A Psychoanalytic Approach to Aesthetic Form.* Madison, CN: International Universities Press.

Rose, G. J. (1993). On form and feeling in music. In: S. Feder, R. Karmel, & G. Pollock (Eds.) *Psychoanalytic Explorations in Music: Second Series.* New York: International Universities Press.

Rosenbaum, S. (1967). Symbolic meaning and theoretical significance of the analytic couch. *Science and Psychoanalysis, 11*: 182–201.

Rushdie, S. (1981). *Midnight's Children.* London: Jonathan Cape.

Rycroft, C. (1968). *A Critical Dictionary of Psychoanalysis.* Harmondsworth: Penguin, 1972.

Sabbadini, A. (Ed.) (1979). *Il Tempo in Psicoanalisi.* Milano: Feltrinelli.

Sabbadini, A. (1986). Tempo e identità: Alcune considerazioni psicoanalitiche. In: P. Reale (Ed.) *Tempo e Identità* (pp. 116–127). Milano: Franco Angeli.

Sabbadini, A. (2011). Cameras, mirrors and the bridge space: A Winnicottian lens on cinema. *Projections, 5*: 17–30.

Sabbadini, A., & Stein, A. (2001). 'Just choose one': Memory and time in Kore-eda's *Wandafuru Raifu (Afterlife). The International Journal of Psychoanalysis, 82*: 603–608.

Salomonsson, B. (1989). Music and affects: Psychoanalytical viewpoints. *Scandinavian Psychoanalytical Review, 12*: 126–144.

Saul, L. (1958). *Technic and Practice of Psychoanalysis.* Philadelphia, PA: Lippencott.

Schachter, J. (1992). Concepts of termination and post-termination patient-analyst contact. *The International Journal of Psychoanalysis, 73*: 137–154.

Schachter, J., & Kächele, H. (2010). The couch in psychoanalysis. *Contemporary Psychoanalysis, 46*: 439–459.

Schafer, R. (1983). *The Analytic Attitude.* London: Hogarth.

Schlesinger, H. J. (2005). *Endings and Beginnings: On Terminating Psychotherapy and Psychoanalysis.* Hillsdale, NJ: Analytic.

Schnitzler, A. (1917). *Casanovas Heimfahrt* [Translated into English and published as *Casanova's Homecoming*]. London: Weidenfeld & Nicholson, 1954.

Segal, H. (1987). Silence is the real crime. *International Review of Psychoanalysis, 14*: 3–12.

Serani, D. (2000). Silence in the analytic space: Resistance or reverie? *Contemporary Psychoanalysis, 36*: 505–519.

Shakespeare, W. (c. 1592) Comedy of Errors. In: P. Alexander (Ed.) *William Shakespeare: The Complete Works.* London: Collins, 1951.

Shakespeare, W. (c. 1595). King Henry the Fourth: Part One. In: P. Alexander (Ed.) *William Shakespeare: The Complete Works*. London: Collins, 1951.

Shakespeare, W. (c. 1601). Hamlet. In: P. Alexander (Ed.) *William Shakespeare: The Complete Works*. London: Collins, 1951.

Shakespeare, W. (c. 1603.) Measure for Measure. In: P. Alexander (Ed.) *William Shakespeare: The Complete Works*. London: Collins, 1951.

Shelley, P. B. (1822). Hellas. In: *Poetical Works*. Oxford: Oxford University Press, 1970.

Sirois, F. (2011). Termination: The hidden face of analysis. *The International Journal of Psychoanalysis, 92*: 57–73.

Sloboda, J. (1985). *The Musical Mind: The Cognitive Psychology of Music* Oxford: Oxford University Press.

Sloboda, J., Davidson, J., & Howe, M. (1994). Is everyone musical? *The Psychologist, 7*: 349–354.

Solemani, H. (1979). Childhood bereavement: The effects on parents and siblings. (Unpublished paper).

Spotniz, H. (1969). *Modern Psychoanalysis of the Schizophrenic Patient*. New York: Grune & Stratton.

Stern, H. (1978). *The Couch: Its Use and Meaning in Psychotherapy*. New York/London: Human Sciences Press.

Stevenson, R. L. (1881). *Virginibus Puerisque and Other Papers*. London: Kegan Paul.

Storr, A. (1992). *Music and the Mind*. London: Harper Collins.

Tolstoy, L. N. (1886). The death of Ivan Ilyich. In: *The Cossacks and Other Stories*. Harmondsworth: Penguin, 1960.

Vaughan Williams, R. (1936). *Dona Nobis Pacem*. Oxford: Oxford University Press.

Verga, G. (1883). La roba. In: *Le Novelle, Vol. 1* (pp. 292–298). Milan: Garzanti, 1980.

Virgil (c. 40 BC). *The Eclogues* [English translation by G. Lee] (IV: 5). Harmondsworth: Penguin, 1980.

Walter, B. (1947). *Theme and Variations*. London: Hamish Hamilton.

Weissman, P. (1964). Psychosexual development in a case of neurotic virginity and old maidenhood. *The International Journal of Psychoanalysis, 45*: 110–120.

Wilde, O. (1890). *The Picture of Dorian Gray*. Oxford: Oxford University Press, 1974.

Winnicott, D. W. (1953). Transitional objects and transitional phenomena. In: *Playing and Reality*. London: Tavistock, 1971.

Winnicott, D. W. (1958). The capacity to be alone. In: *The Maturational Processes and the Facilitating Environment*. London: Hogarth, 1965.

Winnicott, D. W. (1967). Mirror-role of mother and family in child development. In: *Playing and Reality*. London: Tavistock, 1971.

Wittgenstein, L. (1922). *Tractatus Logico-Philosophicus*. London: Routledge & Kegan Paul, 1961.

Wolf-Man (1971). *The Wolf-Man*. New York: Basic.

Wright, K. (1991). *Vision and Separation*. London: Free Association.

Yates, S. (1930). An investigation of the psychological factors in virginity and ritual defloration. *The International Journal of Psychoanalysis, 11*: 167–184.

Yates, S. (1938). Some aspects of time difficulties and their relation to music. *The International Journal of Psycho-Analysis, 16*: 341–354.

Zalusky, S. (2003). Dialogue: Telephone analysis. *Insight, 12*: 13–16.

Zeligs, M. A. (1961). The psychology of silence: Its role in transference, countertransference and the psychoanalytic process. *Journal of the American Psychoanalytic Association, 9*: 7–43.

# INDEX

Walter, B. 122
Weissman, P. 36
Wilde, O. 110, 142
Winnicott, D. W. 5, 9–10, 14, 21, 126,
    130, 139
Wittgenstein, L. 112

Wolf Man 58, 144–145

Yates, S. 2, 35–36

Zeligs, M. A. 105, 114

Development Identity
Personal boundary.